Why This Book Matters for Young Women

From Him, Not Them is the kind of book I wish every young woman could keep in her back pocket as she navigates identity, purpose, and the ache for belonging. Tracy Harper writes with the kind of raw honesty and spiritual clarity that disarms shame and invites healing. This is not just a guide—it's a companion for the woman who's been performing, people-pleasing, or quietly unraveling while trying to hold it all together. Tracy reminds us that the peace we crave doesn't come from perfection, achievement, or approval—it comes from deep reliance on a faithful God who sees us fully and loves us anyway. If you're ready to stop chasing validation and start living rooted in truth, this book is your invitation.

    —Dr. Zoe Shaw, author of *A Year of Self-Care* and *Stronger in the Difficult Places*

What do driving in Hawaii, chasing approval, and feeling invisible have in common? Tracy Harper pulls together these and many other personal stories and vivid illustrations with a powerful impact: the help you need to find answers to your deep questions. You will laugh at her relatable experiences, see yourself in the struggles she shares, shed tears, and find new hope. Begin to discover who you are and why God made you.

    —Judy Douglass, Global Director for Cru Women's Resources, speaker, podcaster, and author

Tracy Harper's *From Him, Not Them* provides a road map for older teens and college-aged women to expose false guides and lead them on a fresh path to peace, joy, and confidence in their relationship with God. Tracy reveals the core challenges young women will face—whether feeling invisible, anxious, or out of control—and with a wise, vulnerable, and authentic voice, she teaches us how to connect with the Holy Spirit to get back on the road to freedom in Christ. Readers of *From Him, Not Them* will love the cultural lessons from Tracy's time in Hawaii, her honest stories (a broken heart, comparison, and even an eating disorder), her powerful reflection questions, and the free downloads at the end of each chapter (playlists, posters, and more!). This book is perfect for a high school graduate or college girl!

    —Heather Holleman, PhD, speaker, professor, and author of *Seated with Christ: Living Freely in a Culture of Comparison*

Tracy Harper's *From Him, Not Them* is a refreshing and relatable approach to helping young women learn to rely on God in the midst of life's often challenging circumstances. Tracy opens the Scriptures and points her readers to Jesus—the source of our true identity—by drawing from her own experiences and the experiences of others. *From Him, Not Them* would be an excellent resource for a high school or college small group.

    —Cas Monaco, VP of Missiology for FamilyLife, author of *Gospel Conversations Reimagined: A Missional Framework for Today*

In *From Him, Not Them,* Tracy Harper invites young women to break free from the longing for approval from others and walk in the truth that our worth comes from God alone. Combining real-life stories from high school and college-aged women with her personal journey through life's ups and downs, Tracy makes deep biblical truths relatable. She helps readers realize they aren't alone in their struggles and gently leads them toward healing by walking in relationship with the Holy Spirit. *From Him, Not Them* is a helpful companion on your own journey to find guidance, validation, and identity.

—**Whitney Akin,** author of *Overlooked: Finding Your Worth When You Feel All Alone*

From Him, Not Them is inspiring, biblically grounded, and full of relatable examples. It highlights both everyday struggles and deep heartbreak that many young women face today. The world sells alluring messages about security, love, satisfaction, and happiness in lesser things. But don't be distracted or persuaded. As readers journey through this book, the Holy Spirit's flame will begin to burn brighter within them. By the end, they'll feel a passion to take what they've received from Him, not them and pour it out in service to God. Not from people-pleasing. Not from obligation. But from the overflow of God's profoundly perfect love for them. This book will easily spark a new catchphrase— *From Him, Not Them*—a reminder among high school and college-aged young women that Christ is all they need.

—**Kelly Ann Snyder,** founder of Living Perfectly Loved Ministries and author of *Living Perfectly Loved: A Christian's 12-Step Journey to Freedom from the Grip of Anxiety and Fear*

From Him, Not Them is a refreshing and honest exploration of Christian identity for young women. This book cuts through the noise of our culture's identity crisis and points readers to the unshakeable foundation of their awareness in Jesus. Tracy shares with humility and transparency on personal experiences that shaped her personal faith journey and how she learned to trust God as she navigated the coming-of-age years. Thoughtful, engaging, and thoroughly grounded in Scripture, this book offers a compelling vision of Christian identity that will challenge young girls on who they look to for their identity and equip readers to

fully rely on God.
    —**Annie Weber**, author of *Astounding Truths of the Bible: A Bite-Sized Approach to Understanding the World's Bestselling Book*

Tracy Harper has crafted a heartfelt and down-to-earth guide for young women navigating the uncertain transition from adolescence to adulthood. With honesty and vulnerability, she shares her journey—learning to understand the Holy Spirit, surviving a devastating breakup, and trusting God with and through overwhelming emotions. Tracy also speaks directly to the temptations young women face—seeking validation in relationships, achievement, and control instead of resting in God's unchanging love. Through personal stories and biblical wisdom, she gently redirects readers to the only source of true confidence and peace. Woven throughout her narratives are threads of faith and truth, encouraging women to trust God fully in every season. This book is a must-read for any young woman in transition—Tracy's words will be a balm to their souls.
    —**Kristen Neighbarger,** author of *Breathing Again: Finding Peace While Navigating Faith Reconstruction*

From Him, Not Them beautifully weaves Tracy Harper's own vulnerable experiences with biblical truths and practical applications to guide girls and women in navigating life. With heartfelt honesty, she offers a powerful reminder of where our worth truly comes from and how to find strength in God's love rather than the approval of others.
    —**Carrie Watts,** RN, speaker, podcast host, and author of her debut YA Christian fiction novel, *Crisis of Faith*

from

Him

not them

A Young Woman's Guide to Relying on God
for Validation, Identity, and Guidance

Tracy Harper

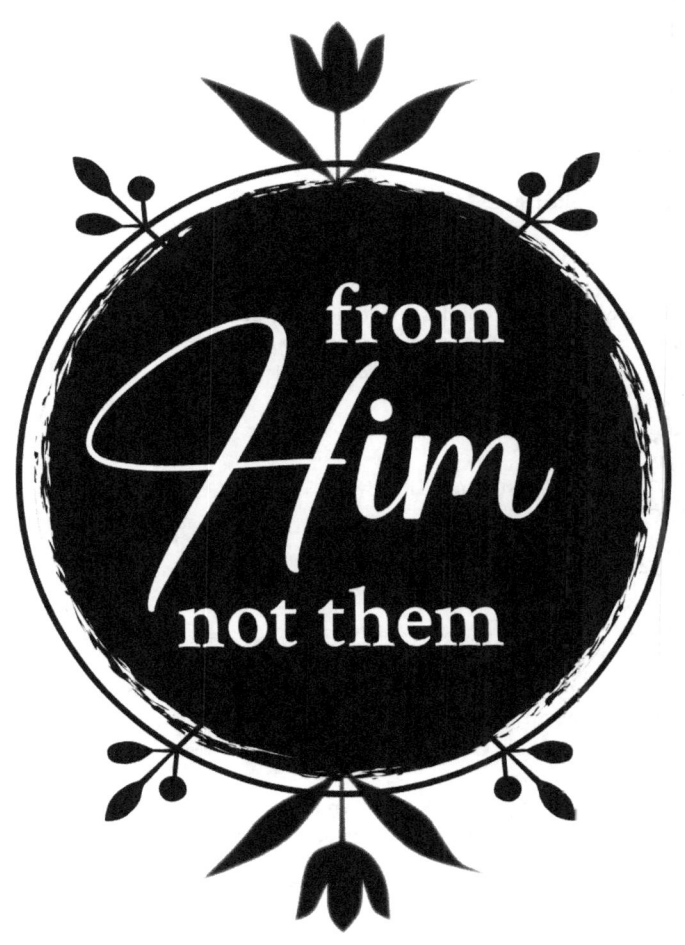

from
Him
not them

A Young Woman's Guide to Relying on God
for Validation, Identity, and Guidance

Tracy Harper

Published by Tracy Harper Press
Preston, Maryland
www.tracyharperwrites.com

Printed in the United States of America

Requests for information should be addressed to tracy@tracyharperwrites.com

First paperback edition.
ISBN: 979-8-9985213-0-0 (Paperback)
ISBN: 979-8-9985213-1-7 (Ebook)
ISBN: 979-8-9985213-2-4 (Audiobook)
Library of Congress Number: 2025907095

All emphases in Scripture quotations and other quotations are the author's.

Unless otherwise noted, Scripture quotations are taken from the ESV® Bible (The Holy Bible, English Standard Version®). Copyright © 2001 by Crossway, a publishing ministry of Good News Publishers. Used by permission. All rights reserved.

Scripture quotations marked NIV are taken from the Holy Bible, New International Version®, NIV®. Copyright © 1973, 1978, 1984, 2011 by Biblica, Inc.® Used by permission of Zondervan. All rights reserved worldwide. www.zondervan.com. The "NIV" and "New International Version" are trademarks registered in the United States Patent and Trademark Office by Biblica, Inc.®

Scripture quotations marked NLT are taken from the Holy Bible, New Living Translation. Copyright © 1996, 2004, 2015 by Tyndale House Foundation. Used by permission of Tyndale House Ministries, Carol Stream, Illinois 60188. All rights reserved.

Cover design: 100 Covers

"It's Nothing Personal, But..."

Feeling the sting of rejection? *You're not alone.*

We've all been there—left out, overlooked, or told, "It's nothing personal, but..." In that moment, it sure *feels* personal. Rejection can shake your confidence and make you question your worth. But what if rejection isn't the final word?

In this free resource, you'll discover how to navigate those painful moments, recognize the lies rejection tells you, and embrace the truth of who God says you are.

Ready to stop letting rejection define you?

Download your free guide at the following website or scan the QR code.
https://www.tracyharperwrites.com/freebies

To my daughters, Taylor, Brynne, and Mackenzie
*You are the young women I had in mind while writing this book.
My prayer is that you will invite God's power and presence into your
life, moment by moment, and experience His faithful love, care, and
guidance in all that you do.*

And to my husband, Tim, the love of my life
*Our journey together in ministry has taken our family across the
globe, and I can't imagine having taken those leaps of faith without
you by my side—as my friend, companion, and co-laborer in Christ.
You were one of the first to help me recognize God's call to full-time
ministry, and I'm forever grateful for your encouragement to follow
His leading, even when it came in an unexpected direction during
my senior year of college. Thank you for always urging me to remain
deeply grounded in God's Word.*

Contents

An Invitation to Turn to Him, Not Them

"Never be afraid to trust an unknown future to a known God."
~ Corrie ten Boom

W hen I was finishing up high school, I knew I couldn't avoid the next big step—heading out into the world and trying new things. But I was feeling more anxious and unsure of myself than ever. Despite my academic and athletic accomplishments, a failed relationship shook my confidence and left me questioning my worth. My high school boyfriend had recently broken up with me, and suddenly, everything I thought I'd known about my future was unclear.

Even though I'd spent months crying, I tried to look as if I had it all together. My good grades and accomplishments masked what I was really feeling inside. In just a few months, I'd be starting college on an academic scholarship with my identical twin sister, Terri. Together, we were going to take on the world! But I was only fooling myself. Deep down, I was a mess, and I felt lost.

My fears weren't unfounded. I used to feel confident in how I handled my life and trusted my judgment. But by the end of my freshman year at Towson University, I was dealing with a serious eating disorder. I had turned to food and exercise to regain a sense of control, but it only added to the shame I was carrying. I was hiding my struggles from the people closest to me and keeping God at a distance. I didn't recognize myself—in more ways than one.

This was concerning because I'd had a close relationship with Jesus since middle school. I read my Bible, attended my church's youth group—where I served on our fine arts team—and even helped start a Bible club at my high school. I went on a mission trip to Ghana when I was sixteen. But despite all of that, I still struggled to feel secure in my identity. Instead of finding my worth in God, I looked for it in the validation of others and in my own ability to achieve. By the time I started college, I wanted God to guide me, but *only* if it meant avoiding any surprises. I craved control over my future, not trust in God's plans.

Maybe you too grew up hearing that you should trust God with your future, but you struggle with that in practice. Life is full of changes and unexpected challenges, and they can make even the small steps you take feel scary. Maybe, like me, something happened in your life to knock you off-course—a breakup, a failure, or a disappointment that left you feeling like you had to prove yourself or piece your life back together. You crave confidence and security, but it always feels just out of reach, and anxiety and uncertainty are your familiar companions.

I wanted to live without worry, too, but I was living in a way that made deep inner peace impossible. I was looking in the wrong places, asking others to meet my needs for validation, worth, and guidance—needs that only God could truly satisfy. Those misplaced expectations journeyed with me into every stage of life—college, marriage, raising three daughters, working with a campus ministry, and even making a big move from the East Coast to Hawai'i. No matter how much I tried to control my circumstances or seek approval from others, it was never enough. The people or things I had been looking to for fulfillment might have met my needs for a moment, but they always fell short and left me wanting more. Through these struggles, I slowly learned that my core longings could only be met by God—from Him, not them—not by anyone or anything else.

Do you find it's hard to move forward to the next part of your life? Does it sometimes seem like life is tougher than it should be? Have you hit setbacks or felt like something's missing that could help you get through life successfully? If you answered "yes" to these questions, you're not alone. We *all* feel that way at some point.

After working with college students in campus ministry for twenty years, I've seen all of this up close. We all have times when we're questioning, exploring, feeling unsure or lost, or even feeling broken. While we may recognize *what* we're feeling, we don't always know *why* we feel that way. But have you considered that primarily turning to other people or things—instead of God—to shape your identity can greatly impact your ability to move confidently through life? This misplaced dependence cripples your ability to move forward—especially when your future feels uncertain.

Take Cassie, for example. She couldn't decide whether to change her major after investing a year in the program of study she'd chosen. Her fear of disappointing her family and friends paralyzed her decision-making process. When we seek validation from others, every decision feels high-stakes, as though the "right" or "wrong" choice isn't just about the decision itself—it's about how others will judge us or how we'll measure up in their eyes.

Then there's Amanda. Her soccer season ended abruptly with an ACL tear, and she found herself not only working through the physical pain of recovery and the hard work of therapy but also wrestling with her identity. Without "soccer star" as part of who she was, Amanda felt like she was nothing.

Or consider Raelynn, who spent her first year of college sleeping around in an effort to fill the void of loneliness and disconnection. Instead of feeling fulfilled, she found herself more isolated than ever. Her need to have a guy validate her worth kept her stuck and unsure of how to move forward.

This crisis of not knowing who we are at our core and who or what to turn to often occurs at a time in life when we face some of life's biggest pressures. And the questions begin to pile up:

What should I do with my life? Should I keep dating this person or break up with them? Should I go to that party? Who are my real friends? What will my life be like after graduation?

And then, after college, the questions keep coming:

What's the right job for me? Who will hire me? Where should I live? How will I make lasting friends? Who should I marry? When's the best time to start a family?

On top of these personal struggles, the world itself presents challenges that often seem beyond our control. We live in a time when news travels fast, and we feel the weight of global issues—wars, pandemics, political upheavals—that leave us feeling disconnected, isolated, and uncertain about the future. One unexpected job loss, a big move, or a relationship change can remind us of how little we actually control.

We all have a limited view of the future. No matter how much we try to plan, the unknowns loom large. With all of this uncertainty, it's hard not to overthink our next steps. We keep questioning the direction of our lives, second-guessing every decision, and replaying every option in our minds. Sleepless nights follow and deep worries creep in, leaving us teetering on the edge, feeling like we're about to crash out.

And perhaps even deeper than the questions about our daily lives are the big spiritual questions we have:

Is God with me? Does He see me? Does He care? Why does He allow hard things to happen?

There's no doubt about it: Life *is* hard. For everyone.

Lexi feels stuck in the middle of her friend group, caught between two feuding friends. While Bella endures merciless teasing from her peers about her weight, Chantel struggles with a constant awareness of her race, always wondering which spaces will feel safe and accepting as she navigates different environments. Jessica's mom passed away during her sophomore year of college—a time when she needed her the most—and she feels lost navigating young adulthood without her. Emily not only struggles with the stigma of being labeled a "drug baby" but also endures a toxic home environment where family members and their friends frequently pass in and out of the house, intoxicated or high.

Resilience and *grit* are often touted as the answer to life's challenges, but have you noticed how often this advice leaves God out? We're told to rely on ourselves—to push through, rise above, and deal with life's problems on our own. But what if there's more to it than that?

Take Sharon, for example. When I met her, she was a smiling first-year biology major, full of optimism, who believed in transformation from within, something she could generate on her own. She told me, "I can reinvent myself. No one knows what I've done or who I was in the past." It sounds empowering—Sharon's belief in self-sufficiency does seem like it could be the key to overcoming her struggles.

Maybe you've been there too. Perhaps you've tried to face life's challenges by relying on yourself to figure things out, telling yourself that if you work harder, try more, or start fresh, things will fall into place. But what happens when they don't? What happens when your strength runs out, or you can't escape the weight of your past?

The truth is, relying on ourselves alone is exhausting and lonely. Sharon's approach of self-sufficiency might sound empowering, but it will quickly become clear that handling life's challenges in isolation only deepens the struggle. Life wasn't meant to be handled alone—especially not when we're facing deep, personal challenges or uncertainty about our future.

Here's the thing: Resilience can look different. Instead of relying on ourselves, what if we brought God into the equation—not as a last resort but as the foundation of our strength? What if, instead of focusing on our own grit, we learned to depend on God's faithfulness, trusting that He holds our future?

In today's world, it's hard to know what's true. We hear voices promising solutions, offering control over our lives and futures, but so much of it turns out to be empty or misleading. We're faced with a lot of noise—many ways to figure things out, but few true paths to peace and purpose.

Are you looking for true confidence and guidance you can trust? Do you want clarity instead of more confusion? If so, I invite you to leave behind the path of relying solely on your feelings, trying to fix everything on your own, or searching for help in all the wrong places.

There's a better way to navigate life's challenges—a way that doesn't erase tough times or answer every question, but reshapes how we think about and approach the unknown. It starts by inviting God into the equation—not just as an option, but as the essential guide for the journey.

❦

Most core subjects in liberal arts colleges typically begin with an introductory course, often ending with the number *101*. Some students try to test out of these classes to jump straight into program-specific courses. But that's not always the best idea. Sometimes, by skipping the *101* level, you miss key information.

Think of the first part of this book as *Finding Your Worth*

101. While you might be tempted to skip ahead, I encourage you to take your time here—this section lays the foundation for discovering your true identity. You'll see me pause throughout the book to ask you questions—don't just skim past them. Take your time. Read slowly, maybe a few sections at a time. Grab a notebook or journal and write down your thoughts. I can't stress this enough: *If you rush through, you'll miss the real growth.*

As you read this initial section, think about where you're seeking your value. Are you looking to others, your appearance, or your accomplishments to feel validated? Just like I did, you might find yourself chasing after things that never truly satisfy. But there's a better way—one that starts with knowing that God sees you and values you deeply, just as you are.

As we journey together, we'll also explore spiritually toxic ways we try to navigate life: relying on our feelings as guides, depending on ourselves to push through, letting anxiety pull us away from God, and seeking guidance from people and places God warns us against. These avenues are counterfeit guides—they seem attractive and helpful, but they ultimately hinder our walk with God.

A major influence behind these deceptions is a belief system that exalts the self as all-powerful. As Melissa Dougherty explains in *Happy Lies: How a Movement You (Probably) Never Heard of Shaped Our Self-Obsessed World*, this way of thinking—New Thought—has shaped modern culture, infiltrating Christian circles and promoting the idea that we can manifest our own reality apart from God. It *sounds* good: Truth is found within each of us, and we only need to listen to our own feelings and instincts to create the life we want. But relying on these spiritual teachings leads to devastating outcomes. As Melissa asks, "What better way to destroy God's beloved image bearers than to turn them inward rather than upward?"[1]

Without realizing it, I had absorbed some of these ideas, and they subtly influenced my own pursuit of counterfeit guides—trusting my feelings, striving for control, and chasing self-improvement as the key to fulfillment. These struggles weren't just theoretical; they played out in real ways in my life. So, throughout this book, I'll share with you some of my toughest life experiences: facing rejection, developing an eating disorder, and struggling with anxiety. I'll also share stories from students I've worked with—some of whom have given me permission to use their real names, while in other cases, their names and circumstances have been changed to protect their privacy.

In the last part of the book, I'll introduce you to a person we often overlook—the one true Guide, the Holy Spirit. I wasn't as knowledgeable or familiar with the Spirit in my early years of spiritual growth, so don't stress if you're just getting to know Him. Throughout this book, you'll see me use both "Holy Spirit" and "Spirit" interchangeably but know that both refer to the same person. God is one being in three persons, and the Holy Spirit is one of them (Matthew 3:16-17). He's our Helper, sent to strengthen us and help us through life. I'll explain how you can activate His presence and power in your life, restore your connection with God when it's broken by sin, and strengthen yourself spiritually for the battles you'll face.

Before you go thinking I'm an expert in how we should look to God instead of others to meet our core needs, let me assure you that I'm not. The truths in this book are life lessons I continually revisit. Just recently, a friend whom I hadn't seen in a long time canceled plans to get together. I found myself feeling crushed and distressed, feelings that went beyond the normal disappointment in not being able to spend time together.

Upon reflection with God, I realized I had jumped to conclusions that weren't true: *My value is determined by how much she likes me. If I truly mattered to her, she wouldn't have ghosted me. Without this deep connection with her, I'm alone and unimportant.* Once again, I was elevating attention and approval from others as the basis for my sense of worth and belonging instead of resting in God's unchanging love for me.

While I still struggle with turning to others for validation and guidance, I'm learning to lean more on God to provide these things. It's not easy, and it's not a one-time fix; it's a continual process of surrendering my need for control and trusting Him in the unknowns. I've seen how much peace comes when I stop searching for answers in the wrong places and start looking to God instead. His guidance isn't always as immediate or clear as I might want, but He's always faithful. And though I'm far from perfect at it, I know that trusting God to lead me through life's decisions, big and small, is the only path to true peace and purpose. I've learned that the more I seek Him, the more I see how He's been faithful to guide me—and I want to encourage you to trust that same faithfulness. Yes, it's a journey, but it's so worth it.

At the end of each chapter, I'll invite you to *kilo* ("kee-loh") with me. *Kilo* is a Hawaiian word that means to watch closely, observe, or examine. In early Hawaiian life, when fishermen went out to catch fish, someone stayed back on land as the watcher, or *kilo*. From land, this watcher could spot fish and signal their location to the fishermen in their canoes.[2]

Jesus was a watcher too. In John 21:1–14, after His resurrection, He appeared to His disciples for the third time. The disciples had been fishing all night but hadn't caught anything. When dawn came, Jesus called out to them from the shore, but they didn't know it was Him. The New Living Translation records "the disciples couldn't *see* who he was" (21:4, emphasis mine).

Jesus asked if they'd caught anything, and when they said no, He told them to put their net on the right side of the boat. When they did, they caught so many fish they couldn't haul in the net! It was then they realized it was Jesus and remembered when He first called them to follow Him (Matthew 4:18–22, Luke 5:4–6).

When we experience limited sight, we need the perspective of the One who sees everything. As we *kilo*, we'll listen and pay attention to what we see and hear. This mindfulness will help us look beyond our surroundings and consider God's viewpoint.

Nobody wants to go through life alone, and I'm here as your fellow traveler. While the future may be uncertain, our limited sight can actually be a gift. It allows us to trust God's guidance through the twists and turns of life. We don't have to worry about every detail ahead—what matters is staying close to the One who is always with us, leading us step by step. Our worth and direction come from Him, not from others. This journey is about trusting Him more than we trust ourselves. That's the heart of *From Him, Not Them*.

Kilo

(to watch closely, observe, or examine)

1. What's your usual gut reaction when things happen that are beyond your control?

2. When you plan for your future, who or what do you look to for guidance?

3. Do you let others know when you're struggling or don't have everything together? Why or why not? Where does the pressure to act like "I've got this!" come from?

4. Read Acts 9:1–31, where Saul (who later becomes Paul) goes from being a feared persecutor of Christians to a committed follower of Jesus. Pay close attention to how he loses his physical sight. What does Ananias say is the reason God sent him to Saul?

Extra Resource

Get your free printable color Companion Workbook with all the *Kilo* reflection questions from each chapter! Perfect if you want extra space or prefer not to write in your book. Open your phone's camera app, point it at the following QR code, and tap the link that appears to access all the extra resources for this book in one place.

You can also visit the following website to access them.

https://www.fromhimnotthem.com/resources

Download Here

PART ONE

KNOWING WE'RE SEEN

1

Limited Sight Distance

> "We have all been blind. We are only
> beginning to see where we are."
> ~ Farsight the Eagle

Before we go any further, if you haven't read *An Invitation to Turn to Him, Not Them,* I encourage you to go back and start there. That's where this guide really begins—where the invitation to turn to God, not to anyone or anything around you, is first extended. Everything in the chapters ahead builds on that starting point.

This chapter is your personal invitation to break free from the pressure to chase after others' approval, direction, or affirmation. If you've ever felt like you're asking people to meet needs only God can truly fulfill—you're not alone. I've been there too. And if you're ready to begin a different kind of journey, one where your value, purpose, and steps forward come from Him, not them, then let's begin—together.

I don't know about you, but medical and dental appointments always make me uneasy. I'll admit it—I once passed out during a routine blood draw, and to this day, I'm on high alert during my semi-annual dental cleanings, praying they don't find a single cavity.

The anxiety starts days in advance, creeping in and making the wait even worse. Over time, I've developed coping methods to manage my dread: if I absolutely must have my blood drawn, I avoid looking at the needles or supplies, I jabber away at the technician to distract myself, and I scroll mindlessly through social media on my phone, hoping the latest memes can drown out my growing tension.

Do you feel the same way? Maybe you've got your own ways of dealing with that pre-appointment anxiety—like blasting your favorite playlist or treating yourself to a little reward afterward (I'll often stop and buy a favorite drink or treat myself to lunch).

My medical visit jitters stem from the fact that when I was a teenager, my first cavity needed a root canal. I was spending the night at my grandparents' house in Pennsylvania, hoping to sleep in on a cold winter morning. Instead, I woke up with a deep, throbbing pain in my lower molar. I'd never had a cavity, so I figured I just needed a filling. But when the dentist told me a root canal was needed, I felt a jolt of fear. This was more than I'd bargained for!

Now, more than twenty years later, I was crossing the Big Island of Hawai'i's mountain range, on my way for yet *another* root canal. At this point, you might be questioning my oral care habits—but I promise, I brush regularly! (Flossing, though? Well, let's just say there's room for improvement.)

As I made the fifty-mile drive, I couldn't help but notice the Wild Animal Xing signs along the winding road. The dead boars on the roadside were a grim reminder to keep an eye out. My friend had even wrecked her car on this road after hitting a boar at night! But for now, the only animals I could see were the ones in the Instagram posts my friend had shown me—huge herds of sheep spilling down the mountainside onto the highway.

This lush island life was a world away from the rural, flat Eastern Shore of Maryland, where I used to live. It was a big adjustment: I'd traded squirrels for mongooses, deer for wild pigs, and ticks for fire ants. Even after living on the island for a while, I was still learning what it meant to live in this space with the ocean on one side and mountains on the other.

As I drove, I talked with God, sang worship songs, and recited Scripture to calm myself. Over the years, I'd come a long way in trusting in God's love and care, even when things were tough. But I was still anxious about this dental procedure. *Would the shots be painful? Could I stay calm through the whole thing? And would it even work?* My sister had once had a dental procedure go wrong, and it ended up causing her more pain than she'd been in before. Her story wasn't exactly reassuring!

As I drove on, a Hawaiian hawk, or *'io,* suddenly swooped down from the sky and flew in front of my car, as if guiding me. Then, just as quickly, it veered off and disappeared. Seeing this powerful bird made me think about what I'd learned about the 'io, the only hawk species native to Hawai'i. The 'io, which is pronounced like a long *e* sound followed by a long *o,* can live anywhere from sea level up to about 6,500 feet. I often heard their sharp cries outside my window, cutting through the softer calls of other birds. Sometimes, I even spotted one high up in a tree, watching for prey like young chickens.

What really amazes me about the 'io is the deeper meaning connected to this bird. I learned a lot from Daniel Kikawa, a pastor and the founder of *Aloha Ke Akua* (God Is Love) ministry. He taught that many Hawaiian words have more than one meaning—they have a basic meaning and also a deeper, or hidden, meaning that can reveal something spiritual.

The bird was a symbol for 'Io, the name early Hawaiians used for their Creator God. Even though ancient chants often mention birds like the hawk or the owl, 'Io was actually the name they used for the Creator—the same God we read about in the Bible.[1] Early

Polynesians believed that ʻĪo guided them to the Hawaiian Islands on their long sea voyage.

Unfortunately, over time, worship of ʻĪo changed, and many Hawaiians forgot about this connection to their Creator.[2] By around a.d. 1200, a harsh new religion with strict rules, called the *kapu* system, took over. It was a fearful system that even included human sacrifice. Worship of the Creator God had to go "underground" to survive, becoming something so holy that people stopped saying His name out loud.

As I pictured the strong ʻio soaring high up in the sky—almost out of sight but still there, tracing my path as I drove across the island—it reminded me that God is also high above everything, more powerful than anything He has created. In the book of Genesis, He's called *El Elyon*, which means "God Most High" (Genesis 14:18–19, 22).

A verse from the book of James came to mind: "Every good and perfect gift is from above, coming down from the Father of lights, with whom there is no variation or shadow due to change" (James 1:17). And that made me remember something I'd learned in a Bible study on James with author and teacher Jen Wilkin. She taught that a shadow is only possible if a light source is higher than the object. God, being "the Father of lights," has no shadow because there is nothing higher than Him.

I thought about how when I was a child, I loved seeing my long shadow stretch across the ground at sunset. I would play with it, moving in different ways to make it look funny. When the sun was shining, I would always have a shadow, because the sun is always higher than I am.

God, however, has no shadow at all, which shows how unique He is—there is nothing and no one above Him.

Just as I was enjoying these comforting thoughts, I rounded a bend in the road near an old lava flow. My eyes caught on a yellow, diamond-shaped road sign I hadn't noticed before.

Let me give a quick refresher on road signs if it's been a minute since you've thought about them. When my oldest daughter was preparing to take her Hawai'i driver's license test, I had to get reacquainted with the different types of road signs because about one-fourth of the forty-question permit test is about road signs.

When I was reviewing these signs, I came across some helpful advice from a driver's ed company: *Don't get overwhelmed.* There are four main categories of signs: regulatory signs, warning signs, guide signs, and work zone signs. Once you know a sign's category, it's pretty easy to figure out its meaning.

- **Regulatory Signs:** These signs, usually black and white (with some red), enforce traffic laws in a certain area. Examples include:

STOP
PASS WITH CARE
SPEED LIMIT 65
WRONG WAY

Regulatory signs are important to pay attention to, or you might find flashing lights in your rearview mirror! And let's be real—who hasn't accidentally turned onto a one-way street and panicked when seeing headlights coming toward them? (That's my worst nightmare because I'm not the best at backing up!)

- **Warning Signs:** These yellow, diamond-shaped signs with black letters warn of upcoming hazards. Examples include:

BUMP
SLIPPERY WHEN WET
TWO-WAY TRAFFIC AHEAD
PEDESTRIAN CROSSING

In Hawai'i, a unique warning sign is the Nēnē Crossing sign, which protects the endangered Hawaiian goose. Since nēnē often cross roads near volcanic areas, these signs remind drivers to slow down.

- **Guide Signs:** These green or blue signs help us find places, like gas stations or hospitals. They also show mile markers and nearby highways.

When hunger hits while you're driving, you start scanning the highway for a blue guide sign that shows nearby food options. Or maybe you've prayed the prayer of a girl who's desperate for some caffeine: *Please, please, please let there be a Starbucks ahead!*

- **Work Zone Signs:** Usually bright orange, these signs alert us to road construction ahead. In my home state of Pennsylvania, we used to joke that there were only two seasons: winter and construction![3]

Reviewing road signs with my daughter was an unexpectedly fun activity. I'd always considered myself pretty knowledgeable about them—after all, I've been driving for years! It felt like a game, identifying each one and explaining its purpose, as if I were some kind of road sign expert.

But then, as I was crossing the island, one sign caught my attention that wasn't in my mental playbook: Limited Sight Distance. I hadn't seen this one before, even though the Hawai'i Department of Motor Vehicles covers fifty-one different warning signs on their website. All I knew was that this sign's bright yellow color and diamond shape were telling me there was something up ahead I needed to be cautious about.

The road suddenly climbed higher, and as I reached the top of the hill, I realized I couldn't see where the highway was going. My first thought was one of panic: *I can't see what's ahead!* I wanted to figure out what that sign meant, but there wasn't time. Right then, I just had to respond by driving forward s-l-o-w-l-y. There was no need to stop, but keeping my usual speed wouldn't be smart. Once I was over the hill and back on even ground, my mind buzzed with what it meant to have "limited sight" while driving—and in other areas of life.

This thought kept my mind occupied until I reached the dentist's office. I was still worried about my upcoming procedure, but I was also feeling grateful for what God had revealed to me during the drive: He has perfect sight despite my own limited vision. Although I couldn't always know what was up ahead, God could see everything clearly.

Have you ever considered how God reveals Himself in ways that are personal to you and your story? In a seminary class, I learned a word that helped me understand God's nature: *transcendence*. It means that God is above creation, completely different from anything or anyone He has made, and not dependent on anything from us. Yet, He is also *immanent*—close, present, and involved in His creation.

My encounter with the 'io reminded me of this truth in a deeply personal way. It opened my eyes to how God's presence can be revealed uniquely, even through something as specific as His historical interaction with the Hawaiian people.

Have you ever noticed how what resonates deeply with you might not have the same impact on someone else? For example, God might reveal His creativity to an artist through the intricacy of a sunset or the vivid hues of a blooming garden. For someone who loves logic, the orderly patterns found in nature or the mathematical precision of the universe might reflect God's brilliance. A bookworm might encounter Him in the pages of Scripture, through a perfectly-timed passage that speaks to their heart. For someone who loves the outdoors, hiking through a quiet forest or looking up at a starry night sky might be when they sense God's nearness most profoundly.

God, in His transcendence, could easily overwhelm us with His greatness—but in His immanence, He chooses to meet us where we are. How has God shown Himself to you in a way that felt personal or meaningful to your journey? Consider the passions, experiences, or even challenges that have shaped your life. Could it be that God has been revealing Himself to you all along, in ways designed specifically to speak to your heart?

When we moved to Hawai'i, God provided friendships with Native Hawaiian believers who have expanded my view of God and His ways. Through them, I have gained a deeper understanding of God from a Hawaiian perspective.

One such friend and sister in Christ, Hālina Yin, is a seeker of knowledge and a healer by trade. As a person of native Hawaiian ancestry, she and her family have made it a priority to preserve and practice their culture. They do this through hula, songs, traditional food preparation, and sharing Hawai'i's history—including its triumphs, struggles, and spiritual challenges. To this end, Hālina has continued in unwavering faith to *ke Akua* (God).

Hālina also had a special encounter with an 'io. While she, her mom, and her sister recorded a hula called *'O 'oe 'Io* (You are 'Io), an 'io appeared and hovered above them. Hālina felt the Holy Spirit saying, "I see the work you are doing, sharing my aloha through the ways I have given your people." This 'io served as a symbol of God's blessing and His presence with them as they worshiped.

Hālina reminded me that, as Creator, God can reveal Himself through the creatures He has made (Genesis 1:20–25). These creatures are not meant to be worshiped but can sometimes be reminders of His presence. Both Hālina and I, in seeing an 'io, felt that God was reminding us He was not distant but close by.

Have there been times in your life when you doubted whether God was truly aware of what you were going through? Perhaps you felt unseen or wondered if He noticed your struggles or heard your prayers. In our pain and confusion, it can be easy to forget that we are not alone. Yet, God's awareness is never in question. His eyes are on us, even when it feels like no one else is paying attention. Let me assure you that God sees everything! The Bible says, "For the eyes of the LORD range throughout the earth to strengthen those whose hearts are fully committed to him" (2 Chronicles 16:9, NIV). He sees every step we take (Job 34:21), knows all things (1 John 3:20), and hears the prayers of His people (1 Peter 3:12).

These truths remind us that God knows everything, sees everything, and understands everything. Even in moments of doubt, He is fully aware of your journey and is actively working for your good.

Take a moment to consider how God might be reminding you of His presence today. Could it be through a kind word from a friend, an unexpected provision, or even a moment of beauty in creation?

Remembering the image of that high-flying 'io gave me the comfort I needed to survive my dental ordeal. I ended up needing more numbing shots than usual, and my heart was racing wildly during the procedure (it would have been nice if someone had warned me this was normal!). Between the tooth pressure, the noise, and the length of the procedure, I was ready to pass out for real. Yet, my experience with the 'io and that Limited Sight Distance road sign strengthened a core truth: *We are always in God's sight, even when ours is limited.*

The transition from high school to the next stage of life can feel like stepping into the unknown, much like driving into a dense fog or approaching a curve with limited sight distance. Naturally, you want to slow down, uncertain of what's ahead. But then, suddenly, life seems to speed up, and you're expected to know exactly where you're going. No pressure, right?

Some people around you might seem to have their futures perfectly mapped out—the ones who chose their college major years ago or come from families where a particular profession is practically a family tradition. (I come from a family of all educators, so I know how that feels!)

But what if your path looks different? Maybe you're the first in your family to consider college, or you're drawn to a trade school, or you want to dive straight into the workforce. Without a clear roadmap or someone to guide you step by step, uncertainty can hit hard. And questions swirl: *What if I choose the wrong path? What if I don't measure up to everyone else? What if I start something and realize it's not what I really want?* It can feel like you're racing ahead blind, unsure of what's around the next bend.

Here's where the insight from the Limited Sight Distance sign comes into play: When we can't see well, the safest response is to slow down but keep moving. Failing to pause and assess the situation can lead to mistakes or missed opportunities. When I first encountered the sign on a winding road, I instinctively hit the brakes. If I hadn't, I could have overshot the curve—or collided with an oncoming car I couldn't see. Slowing down gave me time to process what was happening and decide on the safest way forward.

Major transitions—like the one that happens after high school—can feel overwhelming, and when the road ahead feels unclear, it's okay to slow down. Pausing doesn't mean you're stuck or falling behind—it means you're being intentional. Slowing down allows you to take a breath, assess your surroundings, and ask important questions: *What's God showing me here? How can I trust Him more in this moment? What's my next step?* While the path ahead might not be fully clear, in these moments of disorientation, God offers an unexpected gift: the chance to be fully present, to notice what we might have overlooked, and to trust that He will guide us forward, one step at a time.

In the Marvel Cinematic Universe (MCU) movies, Thor experiences a loss of vision in *Thor: Ragnarok*. During the climactic battle with Hela, Thor loses his right eye. This moment is pivotal as Thor comes to realize that his true power doesn't come from his physical sight or even his hammer, but from within himself as the God of Thunder.

We can relate to the panic Thor initially felt when he lost his eye. When we lose our ability to see clearly, we feel unsettled because, as humans, we often equate vision with control.

One February during Hawai'i's rainy season, my hometown set a record—rain fell every single day for over a month! And we're not talking about light showers, but torrential downpours that made using the windshield wipers on the highest setting a must. When we can't see clearly—whether it's driving through a dark tunnel, dealing with fogged-up glasses, or stepping into bright sunshine and being blinded by the glare—we realize something we usually take for granted: the ability to navigate with ease. Suddenly, we feel unprepared and uncertain how to move forward.

Similarly, in life's unclear moments, we find that relying solely on what *we* can see and understand won't carry us through. Unlike Thor, we will not find within ourselves what we need. This is why Scripture reminds us that "we walk by faith, not by sight" (2 Corinthians 5:7). We require God's help to navigate the external circumstances we face but also the internal struggles that shape how we respond to them. Whether it's fear, doubt, or weariness, God meets us in our deepest places of need, offering wisdom, strength, and peace to guide us through the challenges both around us and within us.

Tara was a brand-new believer when she graduated from high school and started college. She had never read through the Bible, had just begun to understand how to pray, and was leaving her close-knit family to attend college ten hours away. Before she left, the family that had taken her to church during her senior year encouraged her to find a Christian group on campus and told her they would be praying for her.

During her first few days away from home, Tara struggled. She wanted to fit in, felt anxious about who her new friends would be, and wondered if she would find other Christians—or if college would be all about partying and trying to blend in with the crowd.

During the first week of classes, Tara spotted a campus ministry table at an activity fair, and that night, she decided to trust God. She attended the weekly gathering, where her entire college journey as a Christian began. Eventually, Tara went on mission trips, met her future husband and her best friends in the group, and, after graduating, served full-time with that campus ministry.

Looking back, Tara is grateful that despite her initial fears and the struggles of missing her family, she trusted God to lead her to this community of believers—one that felt like home. Her decision to walk by faith and trust God changed the course of her entire future.

God doesn't intend for us to face life alone. When we struggle with our own inadequacies and question our own choices, we can become more aware of our need for Him. And when we're dependent on God's sight instead of our own, we can learn to lean on Him and let Him guide us.

The story of the two disciples on the road to Emmaus in Luke 24 is a perfect example of this truth. They walked with Jesus, who had been raised from the dead, but "their eyes were kept from recognizing him" (v. 17). Only after He opened the Scriptures to them and later broke bread in their presence did they truly see who He was: "Their eyes were opened" (v. 31). Their hearts had already burned within them as Jesus explained the Scriptures, but their true understanding came through the journey, the conversation, and the shared moment—not through physical sight alone. In that moment, the disciples realized they were in the presence of the risen Lord, and it led them to immediately journey back to Jerusalem to share the news with others.

Similarly, when Thomas saw Jesus' wounds after the resurrection, he believed only because he saw with his own eyes. Yet Jesus gently pointed out that there's a special blessing in trusting Him without needing physical evidence: "Blessed are those who have not seen and yet have believed" (John 20:29). Jesus teaches us that spiritual insight and faith bring a deeper understanding and closeness to Him than sight alone ever could.

Maybe today you're driving alone for the first time with your provisional license, and you're starting to feel the weight of the responsibility, wondering if you'll ever get completely comfortable behind the wheel. Or perhaps you just got your first "D" on a test and you feel overwhelmed, wondering how you'll ever bring your grade up or if this class is more than you can handle. Maybe an important relationship just ended, and it's hard to picture the future without someone you thought would be in your life for the long haul (I've been there, and I'll share more about that in the next chapter). We all face moments like these—physical and emotional struggles, spiritual battles, inner conflicts, or situations with uncertain outcomes.

Remember how, on the way to my root canal, God reminded me of His perfect sight despite my inability to see what lay ahead? Through the Limited Sight Distance sign, He highlighted my limitations, but through the 'io flying in front of my car, He showed me His ability to see everything clearly. No matter how clouded our perspective may be, we are always fully visible to Him.

Consider this comforting reality: In times when our vision is limited, we don't need all the answers to be close to God. In fact, it's often in these times of obscurity that God's work in our hearts is most profound. Sometimes, we may look back and see the purpose of past trials with greater clarity, while other answers may remain a mystery. Yet in living by faith, we discover that what we've gained—greater intimacy with Jesus, a softer heart, and a more attuned spirit—far outweighs the clarity we've lost.

When we live by faith, we understand that true vision isn't about what we're seeing but rather about Whom we're trusting.

Kilo

(to watch closely, observe, or examine)

1. Have you experienced a driving situation where you couldn't see well? What was the road or terrain like?

2. Read Psalm 139. In verse 9, the psalmist says, "If I take the wings of the morning and dwell in the uppermost parts of the sea, *even there* your hand shall lead me, and your right hand shall hold me" (emphasis mine). What's your "even

there"—the place in life where you're facing limited sight or uncertainty?

3. In times of not knowing where life is heading, what have you thought about God?

4. What parts of Psalm 139 give you strength or comfort on your journey?

Extra Resource

The reminder *"When You Can't See, Trust the One Who Can"* will encourage you to pause, trust God's perfect vision, and keep moving forward—even when the path ahead feels uncertain. This free poster features a photograph of the original Limited Sight Distance sign that first caught my attention, placed in its real-world setting. Keep it somewhere you'll see it often—a daily reminder to trust Him in life's twists and turns!

Visit the following website to download your poster or scan the QR code below.

https://www.fromhimnotthem.com/resources

2

My Invisibility Superpower

"We are lost, she and I, unseen and not seeing, unheard and not hearing, unknown by others."
~ Amy Tan

Icebreaker games have always been a regular part of my campus ministry work. I've heard people share everything from their biggest highs and lows to which animal they'd want as their spirit animal. And everyone loves the question about which superpower they'd choose if they could.

Students wish they could time travel or maybe fly. And I often say I'd like the power to sleep anywhere—especially on long flights when everyone else is snoozing, and I can't sleep at all! Harry Potter fans usually pick invisibility. At first, it seems like a useful superpower. After all, who wouldn't want to disappear when it's time to clean the kitchen or take an exam or deal with drama?

But invisibility isn't all it's cracked up to be. I was granted this invisibility "power" when my high school boyfriend dumped me (HS Boyfriend, hereafter).

My parents had a clear rule when I was growing up: I wasn't allowed to date until I turned sixteen. It wasn't a big deal since no one special had caught my eye before then. But they made an exception for a boy from my church youth group, who attended a different high school, to take me to my high school's homecoming dance just before my sixteenth birthday.

That day, my high school volleyball team played in a tournament at our rival school. We all wanted to win, but I'll admit some of us were more eager to finish in time to go home and transform from sweaty athletes into glamorous, head-turning dates. Our team didn't play its best and we lost, but we didn't mind too much—there was still the excitement of the evening ahead.

Adding a bit of drama, the largest pimple I'd ever had erupted right in the crease beside my nose. No amount of concealer would make it disappear. Still, I decided to make the best of it and hoped the rest of my look would draw attention away from "Mt. Vesuvius." Thankfully, my date never mentioned it, and he made me feel beautiful regardless.

After he carefully slipped the rose corsage around my wrist, we took the classic pre-dance photos, all smiles and anticipation. That night, we laughed, gazed into each other's eyes, and did our best on the dance floor—even though fast dancing was definitely not our strong suit. When the slow songs played, like Whitney Houston's "I Will Always Love You," I knew I was smitten. *Game over.* It was the beginning of something that felt wonderfully significant.

🌸

Over the next year and a half, HS Boyfriend and I had a great time together. We shared much in common—playing sports, serving on our church's youth drama team, and spending every moment we could at the youth building. His mom was incredibly sweet, and I loved spending time with his family. It all felt like it was coming together perfectly. I imagined we'd be one of those rare couples who met as teens, never dated anyone else, and married young. Cue the wedding bells!

But infatuation blinded me to the cracks that were forming in our relationship. Underneath the surface, we had differences in values and life goals that we weren't dealing with, and over time, I began to feel increasingly uneasy with the direction things were heading.

Yet, the day he broke up with me felt like my world was collapsing. I cried the entire drive home and didn't stop for what felt like months. It sounds dramatic, but I genuinely loved him. I had opened my heart in ways I hadn't before, and now that he was gone, I felt the full weight of that loss.

I grieved deeply for the loss of his presence in my life. For the shattering of the dreams I had tied to our relationship.

As painful as it was, I give him credit for doing the hard thing. He ended things before our connection could lead us further down an unhealthy path. But what I didn't see coming was that he would end not only our dating relationship but also any friendship we'd had.

It was like I'd become invisible.

At church, he usually kept his distance. Whether intentional or not, the lack of interaction—the silence, the avoidance—made me feel like I didn't exist. At times, there was no escape from an encounter. I'd say hello in passing, but he wouldn't return my greeting.

The anxiety I felt over these interactions was crushing. All I wanted was a normal conversation, even a simple "Hi." Instead, I felt dismissed, as though I wasn't even worth acknowledging.

For a while, I hoped we might reconcile. I even wrote him a long letter, pouring out my hurt, hoping he'd understand. I recall one brief, shining moment when I wondered if we'd get back together again. I don't remember what led up to it, but he turned to me and pulled me into a hug. Just for a moment, I felt seen. It wasn't the hug itself; it was that he'd acknowledged my presence. For that one moment, I felt I still mattered to him. But soon after, things returned to the way they were, and I was invisible once again.

Before I knew it, Senior Prom was around the corner, and I no longer had a date. Thankfully, a friend who'd graduated the year before agreed to go with me as friends, and we ended up having a good time together.

But my thoughts couldn't help drifting to how different it could've been. As it turned out, HS Boyfriend was crowned Prom King at his school. Every time I pictured him twirling his date on the dance floor, I felt sad. It was another page from our fairytale story that had been ripped out.

A few months later, he started dating someone else, and I found myself in a painful place. I'd been rejected and replaced. I wondered endlessly what this new girl had that I didn't. I knew I had to move on, but I couldn't stop thinking about it. Was there something I could have done to avoid this mess? Was there something wrong—with *me?* Even though I'd grown up in the church, I didn't feel equipped to deal with the creeping issues of self-worth which accelerated during this time.

Many years later, I realized that my need to be seen and valued ran deeper than he—or anyone—could fulfill. It was a longing that would stay with me into adulthood.

When I'm forced to watch a commercial break, I usually zone out or find something else to do. But there's one ad series that grabs my attention every time. Maybe you've seen it too: Patients from all walks of life share their fears about life before trying the prescription drug Cosentyx.

Most of them had been afraid to go out in public because of visible skin conditions. One man explains that people thought his condition was contagious. Musician Cyndi Lauper appears, confiding she was scared to show her skin when she was covered head-to-toe in an outbreak. Another woman shares she believed her skin would never be clear. Looking directly into the camera, they all plead, "See me." The refrain repeats over and over: *See me. See me. See me.*

See me.

There's a unique kind of darkness that surrounds someone going through a life challenge without support, while also feeling unseen and uncared for. Struggling through hard times with limited sight is difficult enough, but feeling invisible only deepens the pain.

After my breakup, I experienced so much. Heaviness of soul. Deep despair. Powerlessness to change my situation. Hopelessness. Anger. Fear that I would feel this way forever.

The pain I felt revealed how deeply I longed to be seen. At that time, being seen by HS Boyfriend was all I wanted. I knew breakups were hard, but I'd underestimated how deeply it would affect me. It tore open an emptiness I hadn't known was there. In my mind, getting back together with him was the only way to fix it. But if he was out of the picture, then what was I supposed to do?

Some of you might wonder why I struggled with this so much. Maybe your reaction would be to think, *Whatevs! His loss, not mine!* and move on without a backward glance. But others of you get my reaction. So, what made me more fragile?

To answer this question, I think you have to take a look at my background. Even in loving Christian families, relationships can be complicated. Mine was no exception. When I was in middle school, my relationship with my dad hit a rough patch. As I transitioned into young womanhood, we struggled to relate to each other as naturally as we once did. Physical expressions of affection became awkward, and I pulled away emotionally at times too.

On top of this, sibling rivalry with my twin sister created an endless back-and-forth of who was "up" or "down." If I got more playing time in a basketball game, I felt confident—until she got a higher grade than me on an assignment. I was always striving to feel like I was enough. Keeping up with her was a moving target, but my goal was always to surpass her. Anything less than being at the top made me feel insecure.

Awkward family dynamics and sibling rivalry are common, but looking back, I realize my devastation over the breakup was about more than that. For someone who had tied her worth to performance, this felt like personal failure—I hadn't just lost a relationship; I had lost the sense of security I had worked so hard to maintain.

So when the relationship ended, it wasn't just heartbreak—I felt unworthy, unseen, and unsure of who I was without it.

In that season of my life, having a steady boyfriend made me feel more secure. His attention and affection covered my insecurities. But I was still too young in my relationship with God to understand that only He could fully see, know, and love me. I didn't yet realize that any love my boyfriend showed was, at its source, from God. I hadn't grasped yet that while God's love comes to us through people, those people are still human—and they can never meet our needs completely or consistently.

Did you know that the need to be seen is part of our biological makeup?[1] Whitney Akin explains this in her book *Overlooked: Finding Your Worth When You Feel All Alone*, writing, "You are not a narcissist for wanting to be seen. You are a normal human being."[2] I felt relief—and validation—learning from Whitney's research that my longing to be noticed isn't a flaw but is biologically hard-wired. I'd just been looking in the wrong places for the attention and affirmation I craved.

To be seen is to be *known*. To be seen is to be *understood*. To be seen is to be *loved*. Even more, in times when you feel anxious about the future, *being seen is sometimes more important than our own ability to see.*

Will Hutcherson, founder of *Curate Hope,* and professional counselor Chinwé Williams accurately describe the feeling of being seen: "It's when you feel understood, or rather, you feel *seen*. When someone can recognize what you're feeling and respond just how you need them to. Have you ever said, *'That person just gets me?'* If so, you're describing feeling seen."[3]

There are so many moments where I want to let others know they're seen too. When I notice a teammate on my daughter's sports team sitting on the bench, I want to call out, "I see you!" When a friend's daughter stands off to the side while her peers chat in a tight circle, I want to tell her, "You matter." And when a friend is passed over yet again for a promotion, I want to hug her and say, "What you have to offer is valuable. *You* are valuable."

In 2023, the U.S. Surgeon General released a report on America's loneliness epidemic and an advisory on the healing effects of social connection and community. Public health advisories are reserved for significant public health challenges that require the nation's immediate awareness and action, which underscores the seriousness of the issue. In his letter to the public, Dr. Vivek H. Murthy shared:

> In the scientific literature, I found confirmation of what I was hearing. In recent years, about one-in-two adults in America reported experiencing loneliness. And that was before the COVID-19 pandemic cut off so many of us from friends, loved ones, and support systems, exacerbating loneliness and isolation.[4]

Kelly wore long sleeves to hide the scars from cutting, a way she coped with family trauma and emotional numbness.

The cutting was her way of managing an overwhelming flood of feelings she didn't know how to express. It became a way of coping with her internal chaos, even though it only deepened her sense of isolation. At times, she even considered cutting deeper to end her life, unable to imagine a way out of the despair. Kelly's pain was hidden beneath her sleeves, but it was no less real. The scars told a story of feeling misunderstood, unheard, and unloved. Like many others who battle silently, she needed more than intervention; she needed to know she was seen, valued, and loved. Acknowledging her pain and rallying around her with support helped her realize she wasn't alone—and that her life mattered.

When we take the time to truly see someone in their pain, it can be life-changing. Being seen is vital because rejection hurts—emotionally and even physically. Brain scans (fMRI studies) show that areas activated during rejection mirror those activated during physical pain.[5] When someone says, "It's all in your head," they're right—but not as they might think. We're not being dramatic; we're feeling real, measurable pain. Remarkably, studies even show that Tylenol can reduce the emotional sting of rejection!

I felt that pain when I was cut from the sixth-grade play (the same one where my sister got a speaking role). I felt it when certain guys in my campus ministry group refused to listen to my Bible teaching because I was a woman. And I felt it when a close friend misunderstood my actions and cut off our relationship, until we finally talked to each other and reconciled.

We're familiar with the pain of direct rejection, but we also get hurt from indirect rejection—times when we *feel* overlooked or excluded, whether intentionally or not. I feel this way sometimes on social media. When I see a friend's large following, I start to question my own likability and feel devalued if I don't get significant likes, comments, or shares.

Often, rejection is not intentional, but it's still painful. Maybe you're at a family gathering where everyone seems to be showing off their accomplishments, and you feel overlooked because your achievements just aren't as flashy. Or you joined a club, but since you don't have as much experience as the other members, you find yourself sitting quietly on the sidelines during group discussions. Or your roommates went out to Waffle House but forgot to invite you, and you wonder if they just didn't think of you—or if they actually didn't want you to come.

Regardless of the specifics, we know what it's like to feel out of place—like we don't belong. It's the feeling captured in that familiar *Sesame Street* song about one thing not being like the others. And when we feel unseen and overlooked, we start to question our own value.

Relationship expert Dr. Gary Chapman says every human being has a deep need to feel loved and valued, even when we don't meet others' expectations.[6] In *Seen. Known. Loved.: 5 Truths About God & Your Love Language*, he writes that every single person he's met has been "deeply shaped by love or lack of love."[7]

Do you ever feel invisible?

Or rejected and overlooked?

Do you wonder, *Who sees me? Who understands me? Who values me, imperfections included?*

The answers to these questions matter because *you* matter.

The concept of having "a person" or "my people" is more than a trendy phrase; it taps into a deep need we all have to be known, understood, and loved. The TV show *Grey's Anatomy* popularized this idea when the characters Meredith and Cristina, two young surgeons-in-training, form an unbreakable friendship. At one point, Cristina tells Meredith, "You are my person. You will always be my person." This resonated with audiences because it reflects a real longing—to be surrounded by people who will support and understand us no matter what.

But what happens when "your people" aren't there for you? The apostle Paul, in his letter to Timothy, expresses his own hurt when he writes about standing alone during his trial—deserted by the very people he counted on (2 Timothy 4:16). And even Jesus, on the night before His crucifixion, experienced abandonment. His closest friends, who swore they would always stick by Him, fled when He was arrested (Matthew 26:30–56). Jesus fully understands the pain of rejection; as Isaiah 53:3 reminds us, He was "despised and rejected by men."

Missionary and pastor David A. Seamands explains that Jesus doesn't only know about our pain—He understands it from experience. Jesus has felt the loneliness, the isolation, and the hurt that comes from rejection. Seamands writes that this divine understanding is crucial to healing: "The fact that God not only knows and cares, but *fully understands* is the most therapeutic factor in the healing of our damaged emotions."[8]

This brings us to an often-misunderstood moment in Jesus' life: when He cries out on the cross, "My God, my God, why have you forsaken me?" (Matthew 27:46). I used to wonder if these words meant God had abandoned Jesus, turning away in His darkest hour. But as I learned,[9] Jesus was actually quoting Psalm 22—a psalm that foretells the Messiah's suffering and ultimately declares God's faithfulness. Bible teacher Rich Schmidt explains that Jesus wasn't saying God had turned His back on Him; instead, He was pointing His listeners to Scripture, saying in effect, "This is happening as it was written." In fact, Psalm 22:24 affirms that God did not hide His face from His suffering servant but listened to His cries.

Jesus was not alone; Father God did *not* stop seeing Jesus—especially in his darkest moment.

One day, while driving through town, I was reflecting on what it means to feel unseen. As I spoke a few thoughts into my phone, the word *unseen* auto-corrected to *on scene*. I felt God speaking to me in that moment: *You may feel unseen, but I am on scene.*

It was a powerful reminder. Even when we feel overlooked by others—when our friends, family, or peers don't notice or value us, God is present: He's on the scene, fully aware of our struggles, whether we're dealing with loneliness, rejection, or the everyday moments of life. When we stop looking to others for our worth and validation and instead focus on God's unwavering presence and love, we discover the guidance and identity we've been searching for. God's "on-scene" presence assures us we are seen, known, and deeply valued—not because of what we do or how others view us, but because of who we are to Him.

Kilo

(to watch closely, observe, or examine)

1. If you could have a superpower, what would it be, and why?

2. Think of a time when you felt invisible or left out. What happened? Did it make you question your worth?

3. How would you define "being seen"? Who or what helps you feel seen?

4. Read Matthew 26:30–56. Which parts of Jesus' experience in Gethsemane stand out to you? How does it encourage you to know Jesus understands our struggles (Hebrews 4:15)?

Extra Resource

I've put together a playlist of songs that will remind you to find your worth in God. You'll have a curated selection of songs that serve as a reminder of God's presence in your life, even when you feel unseen. Each track provides an uplifting soundtrack during moments of doubt or loneliness. With music that speaks to your heart, you'll find comfort and strength in knowing that God is always with you.

Visit the following website to get your playlist or scan the QR code below.

https://www.fromhimnotthem.com/resources

3

The God Who Sees

**"Perhaps you've tried to outrun lack and
limitation with your own resources ... God
desires for you to rediscover, or realize for the
first time, that He alone is your sustainer."
~ Ruth Chou Simons**

I love a good treasure hunt! When I was young, I
remember searching through new-construction rubble in
my neighborhood, looking for empty Camel cigarette packs.
Sometimes, they had a ticket called "Camel Cash" on the back. It
wasn't real money, but the image of a camel with palm trees and a
pyramid printed on it looked exotic and exciting to me.

As a young girl, I also collected things like coins, baseball
cards, and stamps, even though they never became valuable. When
I found out that my husband, Tim's, family lived on a farm, I
imagined all the "treasures" that might be buried there. For Tim's
birthday one year, the family bought him a metal detector. He
hasn't used it as much as I have, though!

A few times each summer, I pull the metal detector out of
storage, grab a shovel, and start searching. The beeping sound it
makes when it finds something is so exciting! The detector's screen
even tells me if it has found metal that might be worth something.

Back in the 1970s, Tim's dad found a Civil War–era bayonet
on the farm while planting flowers. He discovered it by accident,

so I wondered what we might find if we actually tried to locate something. If there was real treasure, I was going to find it!

One day, I finally found something valuable. Tim's brother and his wife were remodeling an old house on the farm. After workers lifted the house to dig a new basement, I searched the dirt with my metal detector. *Beep! Beep!* Soon, I was holding an old coin called a Matron Head cent (from 1816–1839). It wasn't in great shape because it's mostly made of copper, but I was still thrilled to have found one of America's first coins.

Here's what I've learned about hidden treasure: A valuable thing isn't truly valuable until someone finds it. When something is hidden, its worth is there, but no one can see or appreciate it.

But when it's discovered, its value is clear for everyone to see.

You're not alone in wanting to feel seen, valued, known, and loved. Many people in the Bible had a strong desire to feel noticed and valued by God. In fact, God calls His people His "special treasure" (Exodus 19:5) and reaches out to show them they are worth something to Him.

In Genesis, we read about a man named Abram, with whom God made a special promise. God told Abram He would make a great nation from his family, and through that nation, the whole world would be blessed (Genesis 12:1–3). Abram didn't know that his descendant would eventually be Jesus Christ, who would come almost two thousand years later.

Abram was seventy-five, and his wife, Sarai, was sixty-five when God promised them a child. Imagine their surprise! Abram trusted God and obeyed by moving over six hundred miles to a new land. God even changed Abram's name to Abraham, meaning "Father of Many," as a reminder of His promise (Genesis 17:5). God also gave Sarai a new name, Sarah, which means "Princess"

(v. 16) since she would be the mother of kings.

Names meant a lot back then—and even today, names are important. Sometimes, your family name is passed down through the generations. Other times, your parents pick a name they simply like. Names can also reflect a place or item that holds special meaning to them. I met an Afghan student whose name meant "seashell," chosen for its beauty in Arabic culture. Another student was named after a Hawaiian beach her parents had visited and loved. Many Hawaiian names reflect Hawaii's beauty, like *Pua*, meaning "flower," and *Kaia*, meaning "the sea."

Names can also reflect spiritual identity or destiny. For example, many girls are named Rachel, Elizabeth, or Hannah because their parents felt led by God to choose names from the Bible, symbolizing a desired character trait or their commitment to God. A clear example of spiritual purpose is seen in the changing of Abraham's and Sarah's names in the Bible.

And speaking of Abraham and Sarah, let's get back to their story. Ten years passed, and they were still waiting for their promised child. Sarah may have lost hope, so she suggested Abraham have a child with her Egyptian servant, Hagar. In those times, this was a common practice.[1]

Abraham agreed, and Hagar soon became pregnant. But when she did, things got tense between her and Sarah. Hagar began to look down on Sarah, and when Sarah asked Abraham to step in, he refused to take responsibility. This, of course, only made Sarah even more upset.

The drama continued when Hagar ran away. She decided to head back to Egypt, where she had family, hoping for a fresh start.[2] She had been feeling unseen and mistreated by Sarah, and she didn't want to live a life where she wasn't valued.

In her time of need, an angel of the Lord who some think was actually Jesus making an Old Testament appearance, found Hagar by a spring in the desert. He said, "Hagar, servant of Sarai, where have you come from and where are you going?" (Genesis 16:8).

This question, simple yet profound, marks a turning point for Hagar. It wasn't just about her physical location; it was about her heart, her identity, and her future. God's question invited Hagar to pause, reflect, and consider where she had been and where she was going. It's the same invitation He offers us when we feel lost or overwhelmed. Through this exchange, Hagar began to see that the God who knew her also cared deeply for her.

Let's take a closer look at the angel's words to Hagar and see how they reveal the depth of God's love and understanding. The angel's first words to Hagar reveal something incredible about God's character—He saw her, knew her, and valued her enough to call her by name: *Hagar.*

God didn't just find Hagar by accident—she wasn't some random woman He happened to find on a magic carpet ride through the desert. He came to her at exactly the right time and called her by her name. God wanted Hagar to know He knew her and cared about her, even though she felt invisible.

I once felt this way at my local library. As I waited in line, a librarian came up to me with the book I'd reserved, calling me by name. I hadn't realized I was recognized there. It was a small thing, but it felt special—like being seen and known in a place where I didn't expect it.

Hagar's name means "flight," which perfectly reflects what she was going through. Many of us, myself included, sometimes feel the urge to run away when faced with tough situations. When we don't know what else to do, leaving can feel like the easiest option. Don't like the conversation you're in? Just say, "Peace out!" and walk away. But what happens when you're in a situation you can't simply escape—like an unhealthy family environment? Sure, you can hang out at friends' houses for a while, but eventually, you have to go home.

Sometimes, we feel stuck in situations where we lack the knowledge, power, or resources to make a change. Adrienne felt trapped because her mom constantly criticized and nagged her, leaving her feeling inadequate and drained. Gina's experience was even more overwhelming—she endured abuse from her dad. She didn't know where to turn, who to trust, or how to get help. Paralyzed by fear and uncertainty, Gina doubted anyone would believe her, and the weight of her situation felt impossible to bear.

In other cases, the escape we crave isn't physical—it's emotional. Andrea turned to marijuana and THC-laced products, thinking they would ease the relentless pressure she felt at school. Julia spent her weekends partying, getting drunk, and blacking out, hoping to forget her stress, even temporarily. Kara, on the other hand, vaped throughout the day as a way to manage anxiety, even though it didn't address her deeper struggles.

Just like Adrienne, Gina, Andrea, Julia, and Kara, Hagar found herself in a situation that felt impossible. She was powerless, overlooked, and likely overwhelmed with fear. But Hagar's story is different because it doesn't end with her being stuck. One Bible scholar points out that this story is unique: It's the only place in ancient writings where a god/deity addresses a woman by name.[3] In those times, women, especially servants, had few rights and were often seen as less important than men.[4]

When you read the full Genesis narrative, you might notice that neither Sarah or Abraham ever refers to Hagar by her name.[5] Hagar's eternally "the servant." Even over a decade later, when the conflict between Sarah and Hagar comes to a boiling point (Genesis 21), Hagar is still only "the slave woman" (which, to be honest, is even more of a demeaning title).

So, when God calls Hagar by *her name*, He brings her into the light and shows her that she's valuable. God's early interaction with Hagar reminds us that He sees and values each of us, no matter how messy or difficult our lives may get.

Monica grew up in church, learning Bible stories and singing about God's love. But as she got older, she started to believe lies about herself. She thought her worth depended on her accomplishments and being good enough to earn others' approval.

The pressure was overwhelming, and even as a child, she tried to cope by taking appetite suppressants. In high school, things got worse—she turned to laxatives and starving herself. By her early twenties, the weight of it all pushed her into rebellion and self-destruction. She started binging and purging, smoking, and seeking comfort in unhealthy relationships. Food and alcohol became her way to numb the pain.

Self-help books only added to her confusion, telling her she had to rely on herself when she already felt so lost. Eventually, Monica hit rock bottom. She went through a divorce, nearly lost her job, and pushed away her friends and family. She honestly didn't think she'd make it to thirty.

But God is faithful! He never gave up on Monica, even as broken as she was. He led her to a church where people showed her the love and acceptance of Jesus. Their kindness helped break down her walls of fear, shame, and guilt. As she fell in love with Jesus, Monica experienced a joy and peace she had never known. She realized that God had always been with her, even when she couldn't fully see Him.

And God didn't stop there. He continued to restore her life and gave her a second chance at marriage. On a mission trip to Mexico, she met Dan, who became her husband. Today, they have two children. Monica says Jesus is still her Good Shepherd, guiding her and gently bringing her back when she strays.

❧

What the angel says next to Hagar is striking—it reveals how deeply God knows the intimate details of our lives, even the parts others might overlook or never know. *"Hagar..."* says the angel. *"Servant of Sarai..."*

Have you ever felt like you're mostly known for being associated with someone else, rather than seen for who you really are? Maybe you have a sibling who seems to get all the attention, or maybe you know what it's like to feel overshadowed by a friend who's always achieving something big.

There have been times when I've felt like this. For example, growing up with a twin sister, people would often say, "Oh, you're Terri's twin!" Yes, I'm her twin, and I love that connection! But sometimes, I wanted to be recognized for who I was beyond being a twin and appreciated for everything that made me unique. I'm sure you can relate—you're more than any one role or label people place on you.

We don't want to be defined by just one role, but it's important to remember that God sees us fully, even in those roles that feel limiting to us. For instance, you might feel stuck in the title of "Babysitter to My Younger Siblings." Or maybe you're known as "The One Who's Always Organizing Youth Group Events." Perhaps it's "Barista at the Coffee Shop" or "Friendly Student Who's Always Helping Others with Their Homework." Even when these roles seem to overshadow everything else about you, God values and sees the whole person behind the label.

We long to know that someone understands our daily lives, the sacrifices we make, and the unique challenges we face. Anyone who has ever worked on a difficult group project understands the personal stress and responsibility on one person when others don't contribute. Even when it seems like no one else sees or appreciates our effort, God does, and He values every part of who we are.

When I was in college, I had a job as a waitress at a restaurant near Hershey Park, close to all the tourist action. Busy summer days were intense—tired families with little kids would pour in for breakfast, leaving behind a trail of spilled cereal, sticky syrup, and, sometimes, stressed-out attitudes. It was hard work! I even had nightmares of being stuck with too many tables at once, trying to keep up, only to end up with no tips at all. At times, I wondered if anyone ever saw me for the actual person I was other than someone who only existed to clean up the Froot Loops that crazy kids tossed under the table.

I imagine Hagar must have felt overwhelmingly unseen in her hard work and in her relationship with Sarah. We don't know much about Hagar's past, but it's unlikely she wanted to be a servant in a foreign place, taking orders day after day.

Many of us, too, find ourselves in roles or situations we might not have chosen if we'd had other options. Like the young woman who joins ROTC in college to secure a scholarship and avoid overwhelming student debt, the student who gives up their dream school because their parents think it's too far away, or the teenager working weekends instead of hanging out with friends to support their family. Maybe it's the girl who steps into the role of caregiver for a younger sibling, or the gifted student pressured by parents to excel academically and pursue a high-paying career they don't actually want.

Just like us, Hagar found herself in a role she wouldn't have chosen, facing challenges she couldn't easily escape. Yet, God saw her. He understood everything she was going through as Sarah's servant and didn't ignore the difficulty of her situation. Even though she must have felt isolated, Hagar was not invisible to God, and neither are you.

The angel's final words to Hagar aren't just a question—they're an invitation. In just a few words, God reveals His deep understanding of Hagar's past and His concern for her future, challenging her to reflect and trust His guidance: *"Hagar... Servant of Sarai... Where have you come from, and where are you going?"*

Have you ever been doing something you weren't supposed to and someone asks you, "What are you doing?" even though they obviously already know? Maybe you ate the leftovers that weren't yours or lied about something or gossiped about a friend. You're given a chance to explain, to be honest, and maybe to own up to whatever it was. Behind their question—which is probably making you sweat—there's love and a reminder that they see you and want to understand you. Being caught doing something isn't always bad.

The angel of the Lord finds Hagar in a similar situation, at an intersection between her comings and goings, between running away and considering a return to her former life. Physically, she's looking for water, desperate to survive. But spiritually, Hagar has a much deeper thirst for something she may not even recognize—a longing to be seen, understood, and loved.

When the angel asks Hagar where she's going, she answers honestly: She's running away from Sarah. The angel's response is unexpected—He tells her to return. Imagine how hard that must have been! We don't know if there was a long pause here, but Hagar faced a decision. She could either obey and go back or keep heading in the other direction.

If you're like me, obedience to God is not always immediate. Sometimes, I like to weigh my options and calculate the "cost." For example, I've felt God prompting me to stop watching a TV series because its content didn't glorify Him. Every episode was full of foul language, inappropriate scenes, or glorification of behaviors the Bible clearly warns against. Yet I hesitated, telling myself I was just watching for the story or the humor, trying to reason that the "good" in the series outweighed the "bad."

When has God instructed you to do something, and you've delayed in obeying? Delaney wrestled with the choice to stop sleeping with her boyfriend after learning about God's design for sexual intimacy within marriage. Addison hesitated to share her faith with a friend, afraid of damaging the friendship if the person reacted angrily. Maybe for you, it's something different—like forgiving someone who hurt you, letting go of a toxic relationship, or stepping into a new role that feels intimidating.

I've realized that when I finally choose to obey, it's often because I've been reminded of who God is and how deeply He knows and cares for me. I wonder if that's what happened for Hagar too. Something shifted for her. Maybe it was in the promise God gave her, or maybe it was in the simple fact that He knew her name and saw her for who she truly was.

God didn't sugarcoat Hagar's situation or allow her to pretend that going back would be easy. He told her that she would have a son who would stir up trouble, and that life would still be challenging. Yet God also reassured her that He would bless her—that she would have countless descendants, and her son would be a source of strength. God even gave her the name for her son—Ishmael, meaning "God hears," because He heard Hagar's struggles and pain.

Imagine the impact of hearing that God sees and hears you, even in the hardest times. Knowing she was seen and cared for gave Hagar the strength to obey, even though it meant facing a challenging future. The promise of blessings alone isn't what motivated her—it was the power of being seen and fully known. God's attention and compassion gave her the courage to go back.

In a way, we're all like Hagar—longing to be understood and valued, much like the hidden treasure whose worth isn't recognized until it's truly seen. The God who sees knows us by name and understands the roles and responsibilities we carry—roles that may feel ordinary or even burdensome but are still part of the unique story He is writing for us. These roles don't define us, but they do shape us, and at every crossroads, God offers exactly what we need to navigate the journey. Just as He revealed Hagar's value and purpose, He calls us to trust in His care, knowing that we are seen, loved, and cherished beyond measure.

Kilo

(to watch closely, observe, or examine)

1. Is there any special meaning behind your name?

2. Read Psalm 121, focusing on verse 8. Where have you seen God's provision at important crossroads in your life? What do you need to entrust to God in prayer right now?

3. Think about the different roles and relationships that shape your life. Below, fill in the blanks with the names of people or groups that apply to you. Then, choose three words to describe what stands out most about each relationship—whether that's a challenge, a joy, or something in between.

Example:
Daughter – *independent, loved, misunderstood*
(This might mean: As a daughter, I sometimes feel the need to prove I can handle life on my own, I know I'm loved, and I don't always feel understood.)

Now, it's your turn:

Friend – _____, _____, _____

Daughter – _____, _____, _____

Employee – _____, _____, _____

Teammate – _____, _____, _____

Girlfriend – _____, _____, _____

Sister – _____, _____, _____

Mentor – _____, _____, _____

After filling this out, look over your list. Do you see any patterns? Do some roles feel heavier than others? As you think through these roles, you may realize that you sometimes feel out of place. Tasha Jun expresses this kind of tension when she writes, "I've always felt unfit as a Korean but somehow too Korean everywhere else."[6] Maybe you've felt something similar—not quite enough in one space, yet too much in another. Where have you struggled to feel like you fully belong? How do these tensions shape the way you see yourself?

Do you believe God sees you in these roles and relationships? Read John 4. What stands out to you about Jesus' conversation with the Samaritan woman?

Extra Resource

Ever feel like you've been set aside, forgotten, or broken beyond repair? A discarded espresso machine at the dump reminded me of a powerful truth—God sees our worth, restores us, and fills us with His power. That machine, once tossed out and left in the dust, was never beyond redemption in the right hands. And neither are you.

The God who sees you is also the God who restores. He knows what you were made for and delights in bringing beauty and purpose out of what others might overlook.

Don't miss this encouraging devotion! It's a reminder that you are not forgotten, not discarded, and never beyond the reach of the One who created you and still sees value in every part of your story.

Visit the following website to download the supplemental devotion "Finding Value at the Dump" or scan the QR code below.

https://www.fromhimnotthem.com/resources

4

Living for One Gaze

**"If success came in snortable form, I'd sniff it up
each nostril and rub the residue on my gums."
~ Mary Laura Philpott**

Teens are more digitally connected than ever. A new Pew
Research survey of U.S. teens shows that most teens use
social media and have a smartphone. Nearly half say they're
online almost constantly, with YouTube, TikTok, Instagram, and
Snapchat topping the list for teens.[1]

Are you drawn to online spaces? FOMO (fear of missing
out) keeps many of us constantly connected, feeling like we're
out of the loop if we don't scroll regularly. While some content
can be entertaining or even uplifting, the constant pressure to
stay updated turns being glued to your phone into more of a
compulsion than a choice.

In our media-saturated world, it's easy to become
overwhelmed by the number of private messages and emails we
think we must respond to. When I look at my own inbox, I see
emails promoting shampoo, skincare, clothes, and sports gear. I get
travel offers, newsletters from different authors, and even health
tips. These didn't just show up by accident; I gave them my email
address to get free shipping, a resource, or a discount code. But that
"free" deal cost me something valuable: access to me through my
inbox.

When it comes to looking for approval from people and things around us, we're like someone who freely hands out their phone number, social media handle, or email to anyone who asks. We hope we'll get positive attention and that the good feedback will cancel out the bad.

We do this because we crave validation—in fact, we've become a generation of validation addicts. At first, I wondered if this was too harsh to say. But then I came across the book *Her True Worth* by Brittany Maher and Cassandra Speer, and I saw that they basically called it the same thing: "affirmation addiction."[2]

The *Her True Worth* community reaches about five million people every month! This made me realize that *a lot* of people struggle with who or what to turn to for validation. In the book, the authors use a fill-in-the-blank exercise to guide their thinking on this: "I'm more loved, accepted, and worthy if/when (fill in the blank)".[3] How would you answer that statement?

Kelly sent provocative photos and a video of herself in a bra and booty shorts to two boys, hoping for attention. She got attention—but not the kind she expected. The content spread around her high school, leading to public shaming from her peers and a tarnished reputation. She also faced serious consequences at home. While she later regretted her choice, it had a positive outcome: She stayed off social media for nearly a year, giving herself time to mature and learn how to use it more responsibly.

Janny, a college student, had never had a boyfriend and believed having one would prove her value. She longed for the security she thought a dating relationship could bring. But when no boyfriend materialized, she focused instead on feeling better about herself by "being a good Christian"—following the rules, serving and volunteering, and respecting her elders. Although these weren't bad things, Janny's motivation was wrong and she was living as if she had to earn her worth.

Janny's story resonates with many of us. Like her, we can fall into the trap of believing that our worth depends on how much we achieve or how well we perform. Whether it's making the dean's list, being first-string on a sports team, or earning praise for our talents, we often equate success with value. Kelly's struggle with tying her worth to her appearance or relationships reflects another common theme—we long for affirmation, thinking it will fill the deep desire we have to matter. But just as Janny discovered, there's no substitute for finding our worth in God alone. When we stop chasing validation from achievements, appearances, or relationships, we can begin to rest in the unchanging truth that our value comes from being loved by Him.

Yet, because we're so focused on getting approval, we often don't think carefully about who we let influence us. And we can end up letting unsafe or unhealthy people have access to the most private parts of our lives and even shape our sense of worth. Sometimes, people have said hurtful things like, "You're not good enough," "No one will ever love you," or "You'll never amount to anything." And we accept those words as true, not recognizing them as lies.

Clarissa struggled with not fitting in, seeking validation through food, sex, grades, sports, and approval from teachers. She felt constant pressure to perform and grew angry when others rejected her. After her best friend moved away, Clarissa hit a low point and finally turned to God. As she built a closer relationship with Jesus, her anger, temptations, and depression eased. She realized her daily need for God and broke away from unhealthy patterns, slowly becoming the person God created her to be.

We don't need to value others' opinions of us more than God's. Just like unfollowing a profile or unsubscribing from a company's annoying emails, we can choose to opt out from being influenced by people who don't have the power to tell us who we are. Let's not allow anyone change how we see ourselves. Only God, our Creator, has the right to decide our worth.[4]

With God's help and a lot of reflection, I eventually realized that I spent a huge part of my life relying on others—family, friends, even my own achievements—to give me the "validation hits" I craved. I was like an addict, always searching for ways to feel like I mattered. But I didn't always know what to do when I couldn't get that "high" from other people's approval.

One of these low points in my life actually helped me draw closer to Jesus.

My struggle with seeking validation became more evident after one of my first real experiences of rejection. As I mentioned in an earlier chapter, I tried out for the school play in sixth grade. After auditions, I remember staring at the list of roles posted on the wall. I kept searching, but I couldn't find my name anywhere on that paper. It was as if I didn't exist.

To make things worse, my twin sister's name was on the list next to a speaking role. Not only did I not have a speaking part, but also I hadn't even been chosen for the ensemble! Isn't that usually where you end up if you're not a lead but can still sing a bit? I thought surely I could fit in somewhere! I even wondered if maybe the director got our names mixed up. After all, "Terri" and "Tracy" do sound alike, and they both start with "T." Or maybe my audition really was just that bad.

This rejection from the play became a major event defining my sixth-grade year. Every time my parents picked me up early while my sister stayed later for play practice, I was reminded that I hadn't made the cut. And then something else big happened: My dad got a new job, meaning we had to move, and I would have to switch schools.

In those final months of saying goodbye to friends I'd had since childhood, I started having strange stomach pains. They came often enough that my parents agreed to take me in for a test to see if anything was wrong. I remember drinking a horrible-tasting liquid, wondering if the doctor who was watching it travel through my digestive system would find something seriously wrong. But the results showed that everything was just fine physically.

Maybe it was parasites, someone suggested. The next thing I knew, my parents were creeping into my bedroom at night with flashlights to check *you know where* worms might crawl out. As if I wasn't already feeling embarrassed enough!

Looking back, I'm almost certain my issue was anxiety. Today, we'd recognize this as a common reaction to big life changes. But back then, people didn't really focus on anxiety or other mental health issues. Plus, we became busy with moving, and I hoped the matter would resolve itself.

Somewhere in all this change, I got braces. I'm not sure anyone actually called me "Bracy Tracy," but the thought kept running through my mind. I was super self-conscious. In photos from that time, I'm clearly trying to smile without showing my teeth, and I end up looking like I'm wincing instead.

To top it off, I was a late bloomer. Every morning, I'd stand next to my twin sister, Terri, in the bathroom, getting ready for school, comparing myself to her and feeling like I was lacking. Do you have a sibling or friend you compare yourself to? Tania's sister's "unicorn hair" drew all the praise, while Tania's thicker, more tangled hair went unnoticed (though it was just as beautiful). Michaela envied her friend's perfect complexion, and Lily felt self-conscious next to her younger sister who towered over her. There always seems to be someone with that something extra we long for.

When school started, though, I was grateful for a twin sister. Finding a place to sit at lunch as a new kid in seventh grade would have been hard enough, but having Terri with me made it a bit easier. We tried sitting with different groups—the popular kids, the athletes, the nerds, the musicians, and so on. But I never found a group where I felt like I completely belonged.[5]

This time in my life was filled with insecurity. I couldn't put it into words back then, but I desperately wanted the approval of others. How I looked, what I accomplished in school, how I did in sports—all of it mattered deeply to me. And underneath it all, the Big Question loomed: *Do I really matter?*

In losing sight of the land, you discover the stars.[6]

This powerful quote by Nainoa Thompson, a Master Navigator and president of the Polynesian Voyaging Society, captures something important about our search for validation. Thompson navigated across the ocean in double-hulled canoes from Hawai'i to other island nations in Polynesia, without using modern instruments. He was the first Hawaiian since the fourteenth century to revive the ancient Polynesian art of navigation, and his journey has inspired many.

I can only imagine what those first Polynesian voyagers must have felt as they left familiar shores to sail 1,200 miles to Hawai'i. Were they scared? Did they wonder if they'd made a mistake? As the land behind them faded away and they saw only the open sea in front of them, all they had left to guide them were the stars.

As a young teen, I looked to everyone and everything around me to give me value and show me that I mattered, but I didn't really think much about what God might have to say about my identity. Letting go of the usual sources of comfort and validation can be scary. Releasing the opinions and approval of others can feel disorienting. How will we know our worth without their words? It's like sailing into the dark, relying less on appearance and achievements to define our value.

The Polynesians' wayfinding mirrors our spiritual journey: Without landmarks, they looked up for direction. Their example inspires us to seek our way by looking to God. Our new guiding motto can be "From Him, Not Them."

After we moved, I started going to youth group at my church once I reached seventh grade. The youth leader taught from the Bible, explaining how God's Word related to my life. I began to read the Bible for myself, not just short verses but whole chapters and books. Gradually, I realized that my desire to be connected to people, to feel known and accepted by them, came from an even deeper desire to connect to God.

Through reading the Bible, I learned that God the Father loved me deeply! Even though I was a sinner, I was so valuable to Him that His Son, Jesus, died in my place (Romans 5:8). Jesus' death paid the penalty for my sin and removed the separation between me and God, reuniting me with Him (Romans 6:23). Because of this, I trusted that I was now part of God's family (Romans 8:16–17).

I understood I belonged. The Father loved and accepted me.

This truth gave me a new sense of security. I was valuable simply because God said I was. The best part was that my worth wasn't tied to anything I did or what other people thought about me. I no longer needed to chase approval from anyone—friends, teachers, parents, coaches—or feel like my value depended on how I looked or what I achieved.

Of course, as my story will show, I sometimes forgot these truths. I'd find myself looking to people and things again to feel like I mattered. One big example was the degree of pain I felt after HS Boyfriend broke up with me. And if I'm being real here, I *still* find myself falling back into this habit. I realize I'm asking others to meet needs only God completely can.

But thankfully, God is patient. He knew I needed transformation that went deeper than what I'd first understood as a young girl. Each time I forgot, He didn't scold me for failing;

instead, He showed me His love and grace all over again. Slowly, with His help, I started learning to live beyond needing the gaze or the approval of others.

My longing to be fully seen—known, understood, and loved despite my imperfections—followed me well into adulthood. Part of me hoped that marriage would fulfill this desire. But, like many, I was unprepared for the reality that my husband couldn't meet the deep soul needs I carried. Miscommunications, conflicts, and unmet expectations at times left me feeling unseen, sitting alone in our bedroom, crying, confused, and aching to feel my own worth and value.

For years, I struggled to understand the root of my pain. When disappointment surfaced, I would try to fix myself or blame my husband, thinking, *If he would just [fill in the blank], maybe my heart wouldn't hurt so much.* But my expectations were often unrealistic. No matter how much progress we made in understanding each other or expressing our love, Tim could never love me in the way only God could.

During a family trip to the East Coast, we attended the church where my faith had first blossomed as a teen. Walking back into that sanctuary, where I'd experienced countless services, moments of worship, and connections with friends, I was transported back to my younger self. Yet, despite my deep love for this place, church had often given me low-key anxiety—a remnant of unresolved pain from the high school breakup that had left me feeling invisible and rejected.

In those early months after being dumped, my path with HS Boyfriend crossed repeatedly. We'd chosen to attend colleges in separate states, however, so interactions with him became fewer and farther between—especially because his family now worshipped at a different church.

This particular Sunday, I fortunately didn't see HS Boyfriend in the crowd. But God had something else planned for me. The pastor shared these words: "No person can be to you what the Lord is."[7] In that moment, the truth sank in. I was in the very place where my journey of looking to people for validation had begun, hearing the message that only God could meet the needs I kept bringing to others.

Although it would have been easy to lay all the blame on my ex for my wounds, I had to face the truth—*I* was the one with a problem. My need for validation extended far beyond a high school relationship. I wanted the fun girl who everyone wanted to be their best friend call me *her* BFF. I wanted to be so successful in ministry that our partners would feel confident they had chosen wisely to support us. I longed for the influence of my friend who had published multiple books and spoken to audiences I could only dream of addressing. And as I watched my siblings and their spouses climb to new heights in their careers—earning prestigious titles and salaries I would never see—I sometimes doubted whether staying in full-time ministry all these years had been the right choice. Over and over, I had looked to people, to relationships, and to achievements to be what only God could be to me. In each of these areas, I wasn't just striving for success or affirmation; I was searching for something deeper—a sense of worth and identity that only God could provide.

While I've often turned to people or achievements for my value, that doesn't mean receiving love and affirmation is wrong. The Bible celebrates the beauty of relationships and the importance of meaningful work. Enjoying perfect fellowship with one another, the Father, the Son, and the Holy Spirit widened their relational circle to include us. God commanded us to love each other (John 13:34) so that others would see and know Him through our love (v. 35).

We were also designed to work and accomplish things for

God's glory (Genesis 1:28, Ephesians 2:10). Work is a gift from God, and taking pride in what we do is part of His design for us (Genesis 1:28, 2:15). Think of the nurturing elementary school teacher shaping young minds with care, the no-nonsense lawyer fighting for justice, the "git-er-done" mechanic who keeps things running smoothly, the compassionate nurse who comforts patients, or the talented musician who brings joy through their melodies. I know a young woman who is incredibly gifted in graphic design—it's as if she was born for it! Have you ever known someone like that, someone whose work seems to align perfectly with their God-given gifts? It brings God great joy when we step into our callings and use the talents and abilities He's given us.

The issue arises when we look to these gifts—people, work, or achievements—and trust *them* as the ultimate source of validation. In a perfect world, we could enjoy the encouragement of others and the satisfaction of work without idolizing them. But the human heart has a tendency to turn even God's blessings into idols, just as the Israelites did when they melted down their gold and silver—gifts God had given them upon their exodus from Egypt—to create an idol (Exodus 12:36–36; 32:3–4).

When we place our worth in the hands of others or in our accomplishments, we set ourselves up for heartbreak. People will disappoint us, work or school will sometimes fall short of our expectations, and even the greatest achievements will never be enough to fill the hole in our hearts meant for God alone. It's like what Pastor Matt Chandler shared in his sermon *The God of Mercy and Glory*: "Every human soul you will ever meet needs, wants, has to have someone validate it. Like, 'Someone tell me I matter. Someone tell me I mean something. Someone tell me that I am loved.'"[8] When these gods let us down (and they will), we don't know who or what to turn to next in their absence.

"I've had sex with three different guys in the last three weeks. If he looks nice, I say, 'How about you?'" Becky, a college sophomore, explained to me. It was Saturday afternoon at our campus ministry's fall retreat. When I asked Becky about her hook-ups, she said she was searching for a sense of connection and meaning but admitted a relationship with God might actually fill the void in her heart. Although Becky was learning that God accepted her, she said she didn't know how to forgive herself. After twelve years in private Catholic school, she believed she had to do penance for her sins and hope that God might forgive her.

"What would you say if I told you God *does* love you?" I asked Becky. I went on to share with her how God doesn't require us to get ourselves "cleaned up" before we come to Him. He loves us just as we are, all our junk and baggage included.

While Becky continued to process becoming a follower of Jesus, the two of us continued to meet over the next few months. I learned more about how she was using sex and partying—including pregaming (getting drunk/high before going to a party)—to cope with her hurts. But on Christmas Day, Becky experienced a breakthrough, and she prayed and received Christ into her life! Over the next several months, she joined a small group with other women who were exploring a relationship with God. Regularly, we prayed with her to resist the temptation to fall back into her old patterns of living.

Learning to find our worth in Christ and living it out day by day is a journey. In many ways, Becky's struggle reflects all of ours. We're all works in progress, constantly needing God's reminder to turn away from idols of affirmation and instead turn toward God, the only One who can truly satisfy our soul.

Our need for validation—this deep, unshakable desire to know we matter—will only find true fulfillment in Jesus. Our tendency to prove our worth through achievements is deeply woven into our nature. It can take us much of our life to realize that our identity in Christ has not fully developed and that we have often looked elsewhere to satisfy the desires that Jesus alone was meant to meet.

It's a bit like doing the Couch to 5K program. At first, you start with short walks, gradually building up the strength and endurance needed to run longer distances. The process is slow but purposeful, with the ultimate goal of crossing the finish line. In the same way, our spiritual journey stretches us as we grow in Christ. Along the way, we begin to recognize that Jesus' love, His sacrifice, and the worth He confers upon us because of His love—these are our true sources of identity and security. Every other source of affirmation, no matter how beautiful, valuable, or beloved, must remain in its rightful place as a gift from the Giver, not the Giver Himself. When we put other things or people in the place of God, we will always come up short. But if we continue to walk with Him, He will gently teach us to rely on His unchanging love and remind us that only He can satisfy the deepest longings of our hearts.

Do you ever feel like you're not enough? Like no matter how hard you work, how well you perform, or how much you try to keep it all together, you still fall short? Maybe you've felt the weight of trying to meet expectations—your own, your parents', your professors', or even what you think God expects of you. It's exhausting, isn't it?

But here's the truth: Jesus did more than just pay for our sins; He gave us His life's perfect record. When we fully understand this, it changes how we see our own lives and worth. We no longer have to anxiously strive to be "good enough" because His obedience has already achieved what we could never accomplish. As Hebrews 1:3 says, Jesus radiates God's own glory and character, sustaining everything by His powerful command. This radiance of His is the light we live under, rather than the dim spotlight we try to shine on ourselves through worldly achievements.

We often focus on Jesus' death as the core of the Gospel

message, and rightly so, as He bore our sins and took the punishment that was ours (Isaiah 53:11). Yet, Jesus didn't simply arrive on earth and head to the cross. He lived a perfect life in complete obedience to God. Every moment of His life was spent meeting the demands of God's Law on our behalf. His life, not just His death, grants us a new standing before God (1 Corinthians 1:30). When God looks at us, He sees Jesus' perfect record, not our flawed attempts.

You should have seen the smile that came across Maria's face when she understood this truth. As we ate Chick-fil-A, the high school junior and I discussed the depth of our sin and our need for salvation. However, Maria believed Christ's death and resurrection were only part of salvation—about 85 percent of the work. She thought attending church and being around good people would take care of the remaining 15 percent to make her clean in God's eyes. What relief and joy she experienced when she understood that she didn't have to do anything extra to be saved!

This realization frees us from the weight of feeling we must earn God's love. God's approval doesn't rest on whether we "have it all together." Jesus' obedience has already secured God's approval for us. It's a powerful truth to rest in, especially for those of us who are so used to feeling we need to prove our worth or measure up to the achievements of others.

One of the most incredible aspects of the gospel is that it's for people who feel like they can't measure up. You don't have to get your stuff together before approaching God, nor do you need to "pay back" His love by living a flawless life. You are loved not because of what you've done or will do but because of who He is and what Jesus has already done on your behalf.

For those of us who have ever felt like screwups, for those of us who look at the polished lives around us and feel inferior, this truth brings deep comfort. God's love isn't dependent on our success, and there is no accomplishment that could make Him love us more. Jesus' obedience is our proof of worth; His death is our payment in full.

Though I had a basic understanding of these truths when I left for college, living them out proved more difficult. Like many, I found myself slipping into the trap of seeking validation in all the wrong places. Detours became part of my journey as I looked to people and achievements to affirm my worth. The coming chapters will reveal some of the challenges I faced—and the many ways God patiently guided me back to the only source of true validation and guidance.

The journey of living in our God-given worth requires constantly reminding ourselves of what Christ accomplished on our behalf. It means learning to turn our eyes back to Jesus and away from our own achievements, trusting that He has done enough for us. When we see ourselves as already loved, forgiven, and whole in Him, we can be free from striving and rest in the unshakeable love of God.

Kilo

(to watch closely, observe, or examine)

1. Who do you allow to influence your sense of value? Whose words make you feel more or less worthy?

2. How can you stop letting others' opinions or things like achievements define you more than God's? What or who do you need to "unfollow" or "unsubscribe" from?

3. Do you usually focus more on Jesus' death than His life? How might seeing the purpose of His life change how you think about what you produce, how you perform, or how you measure up to others?

4. How can you live beyond others' approval? What are some ways you can enjoy affirmation without idolizing

the people who give it?

Extra Resource

Download a specially designed set of lock screen and home screen wallpapers to help you reflect on the theme of *From Him, Not Them* every time you glance at your device. You'll receive seven beautifully designed images, each featuring an encouraging statement paired with a Scripture verse that reflects the heart of this book. Set them up to rotate daily or choose the one that speaks to you most!

Visit the following website to download your images or scan the QR code below.

https://www.fromhimnotthem.com/resources

PART TWO

IDENTIFYING
COUNTERFEIT GUIDES

5

When Feelings Take the Wheel

**"I rejoice at your word like
one who finds great spoil."
Psalm 119:162**

When I was in middle school, my dad planned an amazing summer road trip for our family. We traveled through several states and visited some famous national parks. One of my favorite spots was Bandon Beach in Oregon, where huge rocks rose up out of the Pacific Ocean. As I walked along the beach, my feet sank into the wet sand, and my headphones kept my hair from blowing in my face. The tide pools were full of fascinating sea creatures, and to my excitement, I saw something I'd only read about back home in Pennsylvania: starfish!

They were beautiful! One was purple, another red, and another orange. These starfish clung to the rocks, and we were so interested in them that we decided to take a few home as souvenirs. My brother, sister, and I gently pulled them off the rocks and placed them in Ziploc bags to bring back in our luggage.

But when we got home and opened our suitcases—oh, the smell! The fishy scent was overwhelming. I hadn't realized that starfish were living creatures, and sadly, they had died on the journey home. Their bright colors had faded to brown. We kept them in a box in our basement for a while, but eventually, they were thrown away.

I still feel a little sad about what happened to them. At least they didn't *see* it coming. Starfish have eyes but no brains. At the end of each arm, they have a small eye that helps them sense their surroundings. Instead of seeing the world as we do, they *feel* their way through life.[1]

In a way, this reminds me of how we often navigate life. Life is challenging, and we instinctively recognize the need for guidance to be successful. Deep down, we know there's someone or something we can follow to provide the direction and wisdom we need. As we've already acknowledged, God wants to fulfill our core longings, but we often look outside of our relationship with Him to have our needs met.

Loren Cunningham, founder of Youth With A Mission (YWAM), talks about this idea in his book about hearing God's voice: "Beware of counterfeits. Have you ever heard of a counterfeit dollar bill? Yes, of course. But have you ever heard of a counterfeit paper bag? No. The reason is that only things of value are worth counterfeiting."[2] How valuable is the wisdom God provides! He wants to care for us, provide for us, and guide us.

Yet, many of us struggle to recognize His voice—especially when other voices drown Him out, including our own feelings. Because our feelings are constantly available, they often become our go-to guide. We hear cultural phrases like, "Follow your heart," or even say things like, "I feel that..." when we're actually thinking something. It seems natural to let our emotions lead.

But here's the truth about our feelings: They're a counterfeit guide. Feelings are powerful and real, but when we allow them to take the lead without seeking God's wisdom, they become unreliable. While they can help us process situations, they can also mislead us into thinking that what *feels* good, safe, or right in the moment must *be* good, safe, or right. That's why we need to remember that God's wisdom is far more valuable—and trustworthy—than the counterfeit guidance our feelings offer.

In the popular *Keeper of the Lost Cities* series, the elf protagonist Keefe is an Empath, which means he can sense the emotions of others as if they were his own. Empaths can pick up on emotions in the atmosphere but must learn which ones to focus on and which to ignore. Translating those emotions is tricky, and Keefe shares insight about this challenge:

> My empathy mentor warned me when she saw how strong my empathy was—that there's a risk that comes with feeling too much and not having the right training. Our mind's natural reaction is to shut down when things get too intense—but *everything* is intense for an Empath. So if you're not careful, you can end up going...numb. You'll still feel what *others* feel. But you won't feel anything yourself.[3]

Keefe's struggle reminds us of how overwhelming emotions can be—not just our own, but also the ones we sense in others. While we might not be Empaths, many of us can relate to the challenge of walking into a room and feeling the weight of the emotions swirling around us. Maybe you've experienced it—the tension of unspoken conflict or the heaviness of grief that seems to permeate the air. And let's be honest: Sometimes, we're just trying to sort through our own emotions. The last thing we need is to carry the intensity of someone else's feelings on top of our own.

It's a reminder that, like Keefe, we need the right training to navigate our emotions. Without it, the overwhelming intensity can leave us either consumed by feelings or so detached that we stop feeling altogether. That's why it's so important to learn how to process emotions in light of truth—so they don't take over or leave us numb.

The belief, "If I feel it, it must be true," can lead us down a confusing and often painful path. For instance, if a friend doesn't text you back all day, you might think she's mad at you, even though she could just be busy or dealing with her own struggles. When you fail a quiz, it's easy to feel like you're not smart enough for the class, even though one grade doesn't define your ability. And on days when you feel unattractive, you might convince yourself that no one else could find you beautiful either, even though feelings like these don't always reflect reality.

This tendency to let feelings take the lead isn't just something we experience personally—it's a cultural message. In a society that embraces relativism, where "living your own truth" is encouraged, emotions are often given the highest authority. Many people rely on their feelings to determine their path in life.

A perfect example of this shift can be found in the 2009 *Star Trek* movie, where the older Spock tells his younger self, "Put aside logic; do what feels right." This felt strange to me because I grew up watching *Star Trek*, and Spock was always logical and calm on the show, even when things got tough. That's why he was so memorable—he made decisions based on reason, not emotion.

But is it really possible to live like Spock in real life? Can we just "hold down" our emotions, like trying to keep a beach ball underwater?[4] You may succeed for a while, but eventually, the beach ball will pop back up. Emotions are like that too—they always find a way to come out.

Carl Trueman, who wrote *The Rise and Triumph of the Modern Self*, shared in a documentary with Justin Folk, "In the West, at least, we have it drilled into our minds from childhood onwards: personal happiness is the key to individual flourishing. I am my feelings. To be happy, I have to express my feelings." This belief—"I am my feelings"—is a tempting but misleading way to live. It may feel good in the short term, but it can end up leading us away from God's true guidance. And we risk being tossed about by the ever-changing waves of our emotions, leaving us unanchored and uncertain.

Nowhere is this belief—"I am my feelings"—more evident than in today's gender and sexuality war. While I haven't personally struggled with this, I've witnessed the deep confusion it can bring. One evening, as I drove a group of teens to youth group, a male student carefully applied makeup in the back seat, occasionally spritzing women's perfume. The girl beside him chattered away about her "girlfriend," neither of them treating these behaviors as unusual. Many in this youth group identified as a gender different from their birth or experienced same-sex attraction, and finding someone who identified as "straight" was actually rare.

I don't share this to cast judgment—far from it. Maybe you've felt the weight of these messages yourself: that your feelings define you, that your outward "you" must match your inward "you," that happiness comes from expressing your emotions without question, and that embracing a new identity will bring wholeness.

I know this is a deep and complex conversation, and I can't fully address its scope in this book or give it the attention it deserves. My goal here isn't to cover every aspect, but to point to a deeper truth: when we rely on feelings as our guide, rather than God, we end up searching for identity and peace in places that can never truly satisfy.[5]

Living in Hawaii has its perks, but from time to time, one is reminded that it's not all paradise. A few years into my time there, I was reminded of this when, less than two hours after falling asleep one night, I woke up to an intense itching sensation in my right arm. It felt like I *had* to scratch it! Had I been bit by a fire ant? I swung my legs over the side of the bed, slipped on my fuzzy slippers, and tried to remember where I'd last seen the noni lotion. Noni is a strange-looking Polynesian fruit that smells terrible when ripe but has more antioxidants than any other food—it's a true superfood.

Half-asleep, I stumbled into the bathroom. There wasn't much moonlight, but somehow, I found the bottle. Quickly, I turned it over and poured the thick brown lotion onto my arm. I hoped it would take away the itch as fast as possible. Then I crawled back into bed, waiting for relief.

A minute passed. Then two. No luck—the noni lotion wasn't helping at all. I needed something stronger, like ibuprofen. So, I put on my slippers again and walked down the hall to the kitchen.

All I wanted was for this annoying itching to go away.

I switched on the kitchen light, wincing as my eyes adjusted. I reached into the medicine cabinet, grabbed the bottle of ibuprofen, and lined up the arrows to open it. Popping a tablet into my mouth, I took a few big sips of water.

There wasn't much more I could do except wait for the medicine to start working. Finally, as my brain woke up a bit more, I realized what had caused the itching—sunburn! I should have put on sunscreen earlier that day when I was outside with my friend Marie. I made a mental note to be more careful next time.

This experience reminded me how big feelings work in our lives. Like sunburn, strong emotions demand our attention, making us feel like we *must* do something right away to relieve the discomfort. Have you ever lashed out at someone in anger or criticized someone because you were jealous? Maybe you regretted doing this after you had time to cool down. The reality is that we often act immediately on our feelings, just to feel better.

When we're in pain, whether physical or emotional, it's easy to forget what's wise. In that moment, all I knew was that my arm hurt, and until the pain was gone, it was hard to think clearly. Emotions can make it hard to stop and think about what's best in the situation. We feel like we have to react instantly, but slowing down and getting perspective can make a huge difference.

❦

When we don't take time to think about our emotions, they end up "leading" us. Healthy processing of our emotions takes some careful thought, reflection, and talking things through with others. We have to start by identifying *what* we're feeling before we can understand *why* we're feeling that way. A healthy response requires naming the feeling first.

My friend Kristi, who is a marriage and family therapist, uses a technique called "Name It to Tame It" with her clients. She also recommends a tool called the "Feelings Wheel," which helps put names to emotions we might not even know we're feeling.

> With the Feelings Wheel, the core emotions are at the center of the circle—which is the easiest place to start. After choosing the most accurate core emotion, you can use your finger to identify the more specific emotions that you connect with on the outer edges of the circle. These more specific emotions are what you can explain to others so that they have a deeper understanding of what you are experiencing.[5]

Because I believe identifying what we're feeling is powerful, I provide a link to a copy of the Feelings Wheel at the end of this chapter.

Psychology supports this approach. Naming our emotions is powerful because it helps us regulate overwhelming feelings. When we put our emotions into words, it creates space between us and the emotion itself, which makes it easier to process what we're going through rather than being controlled by it. This is why so many therapists encourage verbalizing emotions—it allows us to understand and make sense of what's happening inside, rather than simply reacting impulsively.

Emotional processing is like an emotional exhale. Talking to someone about your feelings is how you *emotionally exhale*. Simply expressing out loud what's going on in your heart helps to relieve the pressure. It lets out all the energy built up on the right side of the brain and in the body, allowing it to process out, shifting the energy to the left, where logical processing can occur.[7]

Our emotions give us knowledge, but we still need to be careful with them. As the prophet Jeremiah warns, "The heart is deceitful above all things and desperately sick; who can understand it?" (17:9). So, we need to pay attention to our feelings, learn from them, and ask ourselves, *Do these feelings need any action?*

This is similar to advice that licensed counselor Robb Horner gave me: *Be reflective, not reactive, when triggered.* This isn't easy, though! When my feelings are triggered, my first instinct is to express them immediately. Sometimes, I've even exploded in anger, which feels good in the moment but doesn't lead to the result I want.

It had been a long day on campus, and as I opened the front door to my house, I couldn't wait to change into sweatpants and finally relax. But when I stepped inside, I felt my frustration boil over. Shoes and backpacks were strewn across the floor. Dirty dishes were piled high in the sink, and the counters were completely buried under mounds of clutter. I know one of my triggers is walking into a messy house after a long day, but at that moment, I didn't stop to think—I just erupted.

Instead of greeting my family with a smile, I unleashed a tirade about how no one listened to me, how I'd asked them to pick up after themselves a million times, and how I couldn't possibly relax in this chaos. My words poured out, fueled by my exhaustion and frustration, but as I looked around, I saw the effect they had. My family, who had likely been looking forward to seeing me, now slunk away into different corners of the house, avoiding me altogether. Instead of connection, I created distance. Instead of relief, I felt guilt.

When we're flooded with emotions, our bodies release hormones that prepare us to act. This is known as the "fight-or-flight" response, and it can feel like a surge of emotions.

I learned that it takes about twenty minutes to fully calm down—*if* the stressful situation is over. If not, your heart rate stays high, adrenaline surges, and it's hard to think clearly.

After a conflict, have you ever had someone ask you, "What were you thinking?" The truth is, in those moments, we're not thinking logically—our emotions take over. Aaron Karmin, in his article "How Long Does the Fight or Flight Reaction Last?" explains that our emotions take a fast path in the brain, like speeding down a highway, while logical thinking takes the slower route with more stops. This is why emotions often win before we have time to think things through.[8]

I'm learning to walk away when I feel this flood of emotions, though I'm still working on not stomping as I go! To avoid aggravating the situation further, I've found it's helpful to step away when I'm angry, but I make sure to communicate my intentions clearly. I might say, "I'm not giving you the silent treatment. I really want to talk about what just happened, but I need some time to cool down first." This gives me space to process my emotions without making things worse and reassures the other person that the conversation isn't over.

I also find it helpful to pour out my emotions to God. Often, I start by saying, "I'm so mad right now!" (If I use the Feelings Wheel, I might narrow it down to feeling resentful, provoked, annoyed, or something similar.) Sometimes, I'm so angry I vent to God with unkind remarks about the person—words I later regret, but it's better to take them to Him than to the individual! Afterward, I confess those words as sin, asking God to forgive me and help me reflect His love instead.

Journaling helps me too. As I write, my body starts to calm down, and I feel more able to listen to God's voice. This is important because talking to God should be a two-way conversation, not just me venting. By the end, I usually tear up the paper, knowing that what I wrote wouldn't be helpful in repairing the relationship.

In short, we need to pay attention to (or treat) our feelings, figure out if we can trust them, and, if needed, choose a healthy response.

The relationship between feelings and faith is complex and worth examining, especially in how it affects our Christian walk.

During my first year in college, Tisha, a campus ministry staff member, went through an evangelistic booklet with me,[9] despite my prideful belief that I already knew it all. Yet, I was taken by a note at the back: *Do not depend on feelings.* Bill Bright, the author of the booklet, emphasized that God's Word—not our shifting emotions—should guide us.

He used a simple train diagram to explain this relationship, showing *fact* (God and His Word) as the engine, *faith* (our trust in God and His Word) as the train car, and *feeling* (the result of our faith and obedience) as the caboose. Bright teaches: "The train will run with or without the caboose. However, it would be useless to attempt to pull the train by the caboose. In the same way, we as Christians do not depend on feelings or emotions, but we place our faith (trust) in the trustworthiness of God and the promises of His Word."

Without guidance, it's easy to drift when the emotions of early faith fade. Maybe you've experienced this yourself—feeling close to God at a retreat or worship night, only to return to everyday life and wonder where that connection went. *Was it real? If I don't feel God's presence, does that mean He's distant? Did I do something wrong?*

This struggle is real for so many of us, and it's part of why some people start questioning their faith altogether. It can even lead to a process often called "deconstructing" faith—untangling what's true from what may have been emotional hype. Without a deeper foundation, some conclude their faith was just a passing feeling, no different from the high of a concert or a motivational event.

And it's no wonder this happens. We live in a culture that elevates feelings and treats personal experience as truth. So when the spiritual high fades, it can feel like faith itself has disappeared. But emotions come and go—truth doesn't. That's why we need people and teaching that help us stay grounded in God's Word, especially when our feelings are all over the place. We weren't meant to follow feelings—we were meant to follow Him.

But honestly, we don't always help ourselves in this. Many church programs prioritize excitement and engagement—things that make faith *feel* alive in the moment. Church researcher Ed Stetzer put it bluntly: "Too many youth groups are holding tanks with pizza," [10] meaning the focus can sometimes be more on entertainment than spiritual depth. And while fun can be a great way to connect, it's not what sustains faith when life gets hard.

Because life *will* get hard. There will be disappointments, losses, and seasons where God feels distant. If our faith depends on always feeling close to Him, we'll find ourselves on shaky ground when the feelings fade. But faith isn't meant to be built on emotions—it's meant to be built on truth.

This is where discipleship matters. We need reminders—daily, not just at big events—that our faith isn't about chasing emotional highs but about holding on to God's promises, even when we don't *feel* them. Emotions are a gift, but they're not our guide.

When faith leads, feelings will follow.

After HS Boyfriend broke up with me, I found myself living in the caboose of my feelings, where I couldn't distinguish between what I felt and what was factual. Teasi Cannon, a contributing author to Mama Bear Apologetics, calls this "emotionalism"—mistaking our feelings for facts and letting them lead as if they're our ultimate truth.[11] The emotional turmoil forced me to engage with God's Word in ways I hadn't before, leading to a deeper reliance on the Holy Spirit as my Comforter and Counselor. With His guidance, I began to build my self-worth on God's truth rather than the rejection I'd just experienced.

To anchor myself, I started using a deck of Scripture flashcards focused on my worth in Christ. One of the first verses I memorized was Isaiah 26:3: "You keep him in perfect peace whose mind is stayed on you because he trusts in you." I repeated this verse in moments of doubt, whether I was walking to class or driving. These verses calmed me and helped me focus on God rather than on my fluctuating feelings. It felt like Psalm 119:103 coming to life: "How sweet are your words to my taste, sweeter than honey to my mouth!"

Initially, I leaned on verses that lifted my spirits, like those in Psalm 119. The psalmist, after all, reflects on how God's Word provides strength and perspective, especially in times of sorrow or discouragement. One verse declares, "My soul melts away for sorrow; strengthen me according to your word!" (Psalm 119:28). These words resonated deeply with me after my breakup.

Yet, I knew I couldn't read Scripture solely for comfort. As Jen Wilkin warns, it's tempting to take a "feel-good" approach to the Bible—using verses to soothe an emotion without examining the full context.[12] This can lead to shallow faith, where we turn to God's Word only for temporary relief rather than lasting wisdom. As Wilkin puts it, when Scripture doesn't deliver "an immediate dose of emotional satisfaction,"[13] we risk skipping over it altogether. I had to learn that even when Scripture didn't immediately relieve my heartache, it was still valuable for teaching, correcting, and training me in right living (2 Timothy 3:16).

Living in a culture that prioritizes feelings, it's easy to let our emotional needs drive how we read Scripture. But God's Word is designed to connect us with Him, not just to give us an emotional boost. Sometimes, I read passages that didn't immediately resonate, but I chose to trust them anyway. Over time, trusting Scripture and applying its truth heals our emotions and steadies our faith. When we do this, we build our lives on a solid spiritual foundation. Jesus emphasized:

> Everyone then who hears these words of mine and does them will be like a wise man who built his house on the rock. And the rain fell, and the floods came, and the winds blew and beat on that house, but it did not fall, because it had been founded on the rock. And everyone who hears these words of mine and does not do them will be like a foolish man who built his house on the sand. And the rain fell, and the floods came, and the winds blew and beat against that house, and it fell, and great was the fall of it. (Matthew 7:24–27)

Feelings as a counterfeit guide can be convincing. They're always there, always loud, and often seem right in the moment. But as we've seen throughout this chapter, when feelings get behind the wheel, they often take us off course.

Loren and Darlene Cunningham put it well: *"Guidance is first of all a relationship with the Guide."*[14] Learning to trust God as the ultimate Guide means bringing our emotions to Him—not letting them lead us—and letting His truth shape our responses.

Like Keefe, we need the right training to handle our emotions well. As we practice naming our emotions, addressing them, and responding to them in ways that align with our relational goals for ourselves, God, and others, we can break free from automatically doing what *feels* right to doing what *is* right.

Although I had come a long way in navigating my emotions, I still had far to go. In fact, some of the next years of my life were the messiest! My emotions weren't the only counterfeit guide I wrestled with—I also leaned heavily on my own determination to fix everything myself. You'll see where that got me! What happened next, though, taught me a powerful lesson about what it truly means to rely on the right Guide.

Kilo

(to watch closely, observe, or examine)

1. Do you think that as a society, we allow our feelings to lead us? What about in your life?

2. Can you remember a recent time when your feelings got ahead of your logical thinking?

3. Read James 1:19. What can you do to be more reflective instead of reactive when strong emotions arise?

4. How often do you find yourself reading Scripture mainly for a quick emotional lift?

Extra Resource

To help you identify the specific emotions you may be feeling (so you can share them with God in prayer or with others), use a printable version of the Feelings Wheel using these simple instructions.[15]

A Feelings Wheel is a tool for personal emotional awareness and for spiritual alignment. Just as we are called to be good stewards of our bodies, we are also called to understand and care for our emotional and spiritual well being. Take time each day to stop for prayerful self-reflection. Begin with identifying the primary emotions located at the innermost part of the wheel. Ask yourself, *When did I feel most happy today? Sad? Angry? Afraid?*

Then, ask God to guide and reveal the deeper, nuanced emotions spanning out from the center that fit your experience. Naming your feelings can lead to more honest prayers and deeper connection to God. Sitting with and then releasing your own feelings can help us develop greater empathy and awareness of others as we endeavor to love our neighbor as ourself.

Visit the following website to access the Feelings Wheel or scan the QR code below.

https://www.fromhimnotthem.com/resources

6

Forcing Our Way Through Life

**"An unmet need makes a person sick ...
a need met makes a person well."
~ Jack Frost**

M emorizing and thinking deeply about God's Word helped me start basing my worth on who I am in Christ, not on who liked or accepted me. But when I was feeling vulnerable, I fell into a different kind of trap and began following another counterfeit guide—one of my own making. Instead of trusting God, I relied on my own strength to force things to go the way I wanted.

When I started college, I experienced many of the typical things that come with being a freshman. I was rooming with my twin sister, which was great, but we shared a bathroom with three other girls—that was an adjustment! There were so many decisions to make, from choosing friends to figuring out when to study and when to veg. It was overwhelming at times.

In high school, my eating habits weren't the healthiest—lunch was often a giant stromboli, and candy bars were my pre-sports snack. But in college, I quickly realized how easy it was to gain the dreaded "freshman fifteen." Determined to eat healthier, I started copying what my new friends ate. Some of them were tall, thin, and beautiful, and I admired them. I assumed their looks were solely due to their diet, ignoring factors like genetics and exercise. While I wanted to indulge in the dining hall's grilled cheese sandwiches, made with thick Texas toast and layers of melty cheese, I opted for a plate piled high with greens and healthy toppings.

But this wasn't just about making healthier choices. Deep down, I wanted control—control over my body, my life, and how others saw me. Maybe you've felt that too—the urge to take charge of everything because it feels like the only way to hold it all together.

At the same time, I couldn't forget something HS Boyfriend had once said about my body. He mentioned how his hand felt "a roll of fat" when he put his arm around my side. That comment stung back then, but now it kept playing in my mind. Was this why he'd broken up with me?

My struggle with body image may have started in middle school when I began comparing my appearance to others. It was watered by reflection after the painful breakup with HS Boyfriend. Now, with the opportunity to nourish my doubts, it had grown into the full-blown plant of anorexia. What had started as a goal to be healthier quickly became dangerous. Even though I rarely saw my ex, I thought, *I'll show him*. I wanted a body no future boyfriend could criticize, and I craved control over how others saw me.

At first, I felt powerful. Limiting myself to tiny meals—a packet of oatmeal for breakfast, an apple for lunch, and a small salad with grilled chicken for dinner—gave me a sense of control. When I stuck to it, I praised my willpower. Even though I felt a little tug from the Holy Spirit, I ignored it. I liked this new feeling. When I became thinner than my sister for the first time in my life, I was deeply satisfied. I had outdone her in a way I never had before, and I was determined to keep doing it.

Over time, food became my enemy. I labeled things as "good" or "bad." If I ate something "bad," I punished myself with intense workouts. Once, I went out with friends to Baltimore's

Inner Harbor and splurged on a huge piece of cheesecake at The Cheesecake Factory. When I got back to campus, guilt overwhelmed me. I spent two hours in the gym trying to burn the calories off.

As I lost weight, I started receiving more compliments. I noticed more heads turning and more people commenting on my body. This fueled my efforts even more. During winter break, a guy friend who rarely gave compliments praised my appearance.

People said I looked great, but they didn't know what it cost me. By the end of my freshman year, I was so thin I didn't even look like myself. My arms and legs were bony, and my face had no roundness left. I'd also lost the very curves I'd once wanted. Worse, my body wasn't healthy anymore. I'd stopped getting my period, which could have harmed my ability to have kids in the future. But instead of facing the truth, I kept chasing praise. My worth became completely tied to my appearance.

Even though I thought I was in control, my eating disorder was controlling me.

And if controlling my life was supposed to make me feel powerful, why did I feel so trapped? Food was all I could think about—what to eat or not eat, when to eat, and how to hide my eating disorder from others.

I thought I was keeping it a secret, but it was obvious to others. My sister knew something was wrong the moment she saw me skip the butter on my baked potato—because really, who eats a *plain* baked potato? That small detail exposed a much bigger struggle.

Looking back, I can see how distorted my view of myself was. In a group picture from a dance at the Naval Academy, I'm wearing a blue tank top and a skirt. I remember thinking I wasn't thin enough, even though I was just a shadow of myself.

When I got home at the end of the school year, my parents sat me down. They shared their concerns about what I was doing to myself and said they couldn't let me keep going down this unhealthy path. I felt torn inside, caught between relief and fear. On one hand, their intervention felt like a lifeline.[1] On the other, I wasn't ready to give up the habits I thought were holding me together. I resisted visiting the medical professionals my parents had arranged for me to see. But deep down, I knew I couldn't sustain the effort it took to maintain my current image long-term. I just didn't want to admit it yet.

Have you ever had someone step in when you couldn't help yourself? Maybe they saw what you couldn't—or didn't want to—acknowledge. It's not easy to admit we need help, especially when we've worked so hard to seem strong.

Getting better wasn't easy. It took time, and I made mistakes along the way. I had to tackle every aspect of my struggle—physical, mental, emotional, and spiritual. I learned about balanced meals, sensible exercise, and body positivity. Counseling was essential, and so was spiritual support. Each step forward reminded me that healing was about progress, not perfection.

Maybe you can relate. Perhaps you've felt the urge to push through challenges, rushing or forcing things to go your way. Maybe you've unofficially become the "peacemaker" in your family, constantly putting out fires to make sure everyone gets along. Or maybe home feels so chaotic that you spend as much time as possible with friends, avoiding the tension altogether.

You might be curating your social media presence, crafting every post and chasing likes, followers, and validation. Or maybe you're pouring all your energy into academics—pursuing perfect grades, winning awards, and securing scholarships. The thought of not getting into your dream school? It feels unthinkable.

But here's what I learned: God's guidance is better than anything we can control on our own. The self-empowerment message says we have the power to create our own reality, but chasing control only leaves us exhausted and empty.

Paul reminds us in 1 Corinthians 10:13: "...no temptation has overtaken you that is not common to man. God is faithful, and he will not let you be tempted beyond your ability, but with the temptation he will also provide the way of escape, that you may be able to endure it." The way forward isn't about striving harder—it's about surrendering to Him.

When we stop forcing things and start trusting Him, we find a freedom we didn't even realize we were missing. Step by step, He provides what we need—sometimes through people, sometimes through new understanding, and always through His faithfulness.

What about you? What does letting go and trusting God look like in your life? Where might He be inviting you to step out of your need for control and into His better plan?

Shuffling through the crowded aisles at the farmer's market in Hawaii for the first time, I was fascinated by the explosion of colors and strange-looking fruits. Spiky soursop, hairy rambutan, and pink, scaly dragon fruit were just a few of the exotic offerings. I was even more amazed after discovering our rental home had twenty unique fruit trees growing right on the property.

One sunny morning, our landlord's mother stopped by and invited us to pick some jaboticaba from a tree near her house. Jaboticaba fruit is astonishing—it grows right on the trunk of the tree, not just on the branches! Later, on a tour of a local chocolate farm, I learned this is called "cauliflory." It means "stem flower" and describes plants like cacao and papaya that grow fruit directly on their trunks for extra support. This makes me think of Jesus' words in John 15:4–5:

> Abide in me, and I in you. As the branch cannot bear
> fruit by itself, unless it abides in the vine, neither can
> you, unless you abide in me. I am the vine; you are
> the branches. Whoever abides in me and I in him, he

it is that bears much fruit, for apart from me you can
do nothing.

Do you want to grow in love, joy, peace, patience, kindness,
goodness, faithfulness, gentleness, and self-control? These are
called the fruits of the Holy Spirit (Galatians 5:22–23), and they
grow in us when we stay close to God. I like to think of them as
the "harvest" God wants to produce in our lives.

Laura was known for her determination, but patience? Not
so much. Whether it was waiting to be picked up after school or
wondering why her teacher took forever to grade her paper, she
often felt restless and frustrated. She tried to keep herself calm,
but the irritation would bubble up anyway. One day, her mentor
suggested she pray not just for patience but for help from the
Holy Spirit. At first, Laura wasn't sure what that meant. She'd
heard about the Spirit in church but had never thought of Him
as someone who could help her in the small, everyday moments.

Have you been introduced to the Holy Spirit? He's
sometimes the least understood person of the Godhead, but He's
so important to your spiritual growth! I'll share more about
Him in later chapters, but here's something I've learned about
self-control and the Spirit.

Self-control is a fruit of the Spirit. It comes from *staying close
to God* and letting Him work in your life. The control I clung to
was a twisted version of self-reliance and *not in partnership with
God*. I was trying to manage everything on my own, without God's
help, and it ended up controlling me instead.

My kind of control wasn't healthy. It wasn't about God
helping me master my desires or passions. Instead, I forced
myself into extreme behaviors—like overexercising and barely
eating—because I thought it gave me power. I looked disciplined
and "holy" on the outside, but on the inside, I was avoiding my
pain. The rejection from someone I relied on for validation hurt
deeply, and control became my way of avoiding that pain.

Maybe you've been there too—looking for validation from people or things instead of God. When we do that, we can easily lose sight of Him and let something else take over our lives.

How do you know if something or someone controls you? Here's a quick test: Fill in these blanks with a person's name or an activity:

1. I must _____.

2. I won't feel okay or at peace until I _____.

3. I constantly think about _____.

4. _____ makes me worry.

5. I could never tell anyone about _____.

6. I feel shame when I think about _____.

7. _____ makes me feel powerful.

8. I can't imagine my life without _____.

9. I need _____.

10. I have to hide _____ from others.

Take a moment to reflect on your answers. If any of them bring up emotions or reveal areas of struggle, know that you're not alone. God invites us to bring these things to Him, to exchange our burdens for His peace, and to walk in the freedom He offers. As we take steps toward that freedom, we can also invite others into our journey, encouraging one another and growing together in His grace.

Bondage is not what God wants for us! Paul writes, "For freedom Christ has set us free; stand firm therefore, and do not submit again to a yoke of slavery" (Galatians 5:1). To the Corinthians, who believed they "had the right to do anything," Paul boldly declared, "I will not be mastered by anything" (1 Corinthians 6:12 niv).

Think about what it means to truly live in freedom. Even when freedom is announced, like Abraham Lincoln's Emancipation Proclamation, it doesn't always happen immediately or fully. For two years after the Proclamation, enslaved people in Texas remained in bondage until Union forces arrived to enforce their freedom on June 19, 1865. Without enforcement, freedom would have been just words, leaving many still enslaved.

In the same way, our freedom from sin is both a reality and a process. When we trust in Jesus, we are instantly freed from the power of sin through His life, death, and resurrection. But walking in that freedom—learning to live as someone who is no longer enslaved—takes time, effort, and the Holy Spirit's help. Old ways of thinking and living don't just disappear overnight. That's why Paul commands, "Do not be conformed to this world, but be transformed by the renewal of your mind, that by testing you may discern what is the will of God, what is good and acceptable and perfect" (Romans 12:2).

Disconnected from Jesus, we can't bear the fruit God wants to produce in us. If you've been trying to create love, joy, peace, or self-control through sheer willpower, you've probably realized how exhausting that is. Fake spiritual fruit—efforts done in your own strength—can never satisfy or last. The solution? Reconnect with the Vine—Jesus.

When I was in college, our campus ministry took a fall retreat. On the way home, we stopped at an orchard. It was a perfect autumn day, and the orchard offered wagon rides, pumpkin picking, scarecrow stuffing, and endless fresh fruit. I was most excited about sampling their pies and local ice cream flavors!

Walking through the orchard, I never heard the trees groaning or straining to produce fruit. My friend Lisa reminded me they simply did what they were created to do because they were healthy, well-nourished, and rooted in the right environment. Fruit is a natural result of being connected to a source of life.

In the same way, spiritual fruit comes from staying connected to Jesus. As we spend time in His Word, pray, and allow Him to work in our lives, He produces the fruit. Our role is simple: Stay close to Him. His role is to create the harvest!

When I think about this truth, I'm reminded of those cauliflorous plants—the ones where the fruit grows directly on the trunk. That's what I want my life to look like: fruit so plentiful and well-supported that it grows close to the source.

One of the ways we stay connected to God through surrender is by making room for Him in our lives. The degree of preparation we make for someone reveals how much we value them.

When my parents visited our home in Hawaiʻi for the first time after the COVID-19 pandemic, our family spent some time preparing for their visit. If you're like me, having guests over sparks a cleaning frenzy. (Sometimes, I think we should invite people over more often, so our home doesn't get so messy!) We scrubbed bathrooms, decluttered surfaces, washed bed linens, and swept floors. But we didn't empty drawers or closets to make room for their belongings—they weren't staying long enough to need that kind of space.

If someone is moving in with you long-term, surface cleaning wouldn't cut it. You'd likely dedicate at least one room to be theirs. They'd need closet and drawer space, a place to store groceries in the fridge, and the freedom to prepare meals in the kitchen. For them to truly settle in, they'd need full access to your house.

Sometimes, we're superficial hosts who pretend we're happy that people are visiting but inwardly can't wait for them to leave. We're waiting for the moment when we can grin and say, "So glad you came," then flop onto the couch with relief when the door shuts behind them. It's easy to do the same thing with God. We often treat Him as a visiting guest instead of a permanent resident in our lives. We say we want to give Him full access, but instead we make minimal accommodations, hoping He won't stay too long or disrupt our routine.

Forcing my way through life—tightly managing how I looked to control outcomes and earn the validation I craved—kept me from fully surrendering to God. Offering Him access to every area of my life didn't happen all at once. It was a gradual process.

Sure, I was willing to be active in campus ministry. But when it came to my eating and exercise habits? *Those were mine.* God couldn't touch them. I clung to the power I felt in maintaining control, holding on as tightly as someone gripping a broken umbrella in a rainstorm—even though it wasn't doing me any good. The external validation I received only reinforced my unwillingness to let go.

Have you ever wrestled with someone over the remote control? Or argued about whose playlist to play on a road trip? Or—my personal favorite—had wars over the thermostat? It's funny how such little things can escalate into epic standoffs. My life back in college wasn't much different. I had my hands clenched tight on the "control dial" of my eating habits, unwilling to let God adjust it—even a single degree.

Surrendering control for me didn't happen overnight. It took months, maybe even a couple of years, to fully open my hands and give God access to those hidden parts of my life. But here's the beautiful thing: Even in my slowness to yield, God was graciously at work in me and through me.

That's what happens when we stop treating God like a guest and invite Him to dwell fully in our lives. When we give Him access to every part—no closet off-limits, no drawer locked—He fills our lives with His presence and produces a harvest of fruit we could never grow on our own.

When I was in high school, I was introduced to First Priority of America and its founder, Benny Proffitt. Benny worked to build networks of churches that would come together in communities across the nation and equip teenagers in every school in America to be campus missionaries. He believed students could share their faith more effectively with their peers than adults could.

My sister and I, along with some friends, responded to his challenge by starting a prayer and Bible club at our rural Pennsylvanian high school. Rising before the sun, we met weekly in the physics room, fueled by donuts and a desire to make an impact. The greater challenge, however, was living as a Christian light in a public high school.

Looking back, I am thankful for the training and encouragement Benny's ministry provided. Without that support, we wouldn't have been as successful in starting a Christian club, which continued to grow even after we left for college.

During my second year of college, Benny unexpectedly reached out with another opportunity—inviting me to join the What's Up? America tour. This nationwide initiative aimed to inspire young people to live lives of purpose and faith while addressing the struggles facing America's youth. The project's year-long scope would mean putting my college studies on hold, but I knew this could be an opportunity to impact the next generation of students who were just like me—eager to share their faith but needing guidance and resources.

There was just one problem—*me*! Only months before, I had returned home from my first year of college, still recovering from anorexia. Despite the progress I'd made, I was still deeply struggling. Was I the right person for the job? My life felt like a mess. But I sensed God leading me to trust Him for both my continued healing and my future impact. Little did I know, that year would become one of the most spiritually fruitful of my life.

Forty college students joined the tour, and together we crisscrossed all 50 states, visiting 183 cities. Traveling by trucks, vans, and motorhomes, we lived out of suitcases, ate countless sandwiches, and slept on church and school floors when host homes weren't available.

We engaged with thousands of young people in schools, churches, jails, and community centers. Half of our team worked on the National Student Hope Census, surveying over 12,000 teens to understand where they placed their hope for the future. We gained valuable insight into their thoughts, feelings, and motivations by meeting them where they were—at malls, parks, and community spaces.

Meanwhile, the rest of us focused on delivering programs. In public schools, we presented assemblies with testimonies, skits, and songs, encouraging students to make choices that protect their hearts, minds, and futures—free from the harm of drug and alcohol use and unhealthy relationships. In churches and Christian schools, we expanded on that message, sharing the gospel and inviting students into a relationship with Jesus. For those already growing in their faith, we encouraged them to step into leadership roles, start prayer and Bible clubs, and embrace their God-given potential.

When not in schools, we traveled to churches across the country, urging congregations to unite with one another to reach the next generation for Christ. Along the way, we stopped and prayed at every state capital, asking God to guide and bless our nation.

Despite my eagerness to serve, I wrestled with the dissonance between being part of a nationwide ministry and my private struggles. I feared my sin disqualified me. Although I confided in only a few team members about my issues with food and exercise, it was clear I wasn't fully surrendered to God. I often took solitary walks in parking lots after long travel days, determined not to gain weight from too much sitting and fast food. While healthy eating and exercise are positive things, my deeper issue was the control I was trying to maintain. Although I knew I couldn't hide anything from God, I felt a sense of control by pretending I could.

I didn't realize it at the time, but I was trapped in what is now commonly referred to as *imposter syndrome*. It's that feeling of not being "enough," of not truly belonging, especially in a Christian setting. It's when you know deep down that you're not living in alignment with the image you're presenting. You feel like you're pretending to be something you're not, constantly worried that someone will uncover the truth.

Take Leanne, for example. On the outside, she seemed like the model Christian—faithfully attending youth group, volunteering, and impressing everyone with her knowledge of the Bible. But privately, she was grappling with issues of sexual purity in her relationship with her boyfriend. While she appeared to have boundaries in place, she was secretly dealing with increasingly crossing them, something she felt ashamed to share with anyone. Like so many of us, Leanne thought that if anyone found out, her reputation would be shattered.

Ella had her own version of this. No one knew about her addiction to pornography and masturbation—something that had started from mere curiosity but slowly spiraled into something more destructive. She thought that if anyone found out, they'd condemn her. Every time she thought about God, she felt guilty, as if she wasn't worthy of His love. She felt like a fake in church, trying to act like everyone else, but on the inside, she was struggling to keep the walls from crashing down.

Then there was Jackie, who struggled with something else—stealing. Whether it was small items from stores or even her friends' belongings, she couldn't stop. No one would ever guess what was going on in her life—she had mastered the art of hiding behind a "good Christian girl" façade, and the shame of her secret was overwhelming her.

Imposter syndrome isn't unique to just these women. It's something that so many of us can relate to, whether it's struggling with addictions, secret behaviors, or simply feeling like we aren't worthy enough to show up in church or around fellow believers. But here's the truth: None of us are perfect. None of us have it all together, and pretending to be something we're not only feeds into the lie of imposter syndrome.

Surrendering more of myself to God over time was the key to breaking free from the suffocating grip of imposter syndrome I was under. God didn't rush me through the process; He waited patiently, even when I wasn't ready to let go of the things I was desperately clutching—like my appearance, my self-image, and my need for control. I was afraid to trust Him completely, but when I did, everything shifted. The more I opened up parts of my life to Him, the more I felt His freedom and joy—things I hadn't felt in a long time.

God was exceedingly patient with me, and as I trusted Him more and more, I realized He wasn't looking for perfection—but for surrender. I didn't have to hide my struggles or pretend to be something I wasn't. He was more than willing to meet me in my mess.

I want you to hear this: If you're feeling like an imposter—like you're not worthy or you don't belong—you're not alone. Many of us have been there, hiding parts of ourselves, pretending we have it all together. But the moment we choose to surrender those struggles to God, we begin to experience the joy, freedom, and peace He offers. He is waiting for you to come as you are—not perfect, but willing to trust Him. And when you do, He will meet you right where you are.

I'll give you a heads-up: Surrendering to God often feels like dying, because it is—it's the death of our pride, our control, and our idols. For me, it meant choosing obedience in the small, everyday moments: eating meals even when it scared me, limiting my exercise even when I wanted to overdo it, and offering up my anxious thoughts to God rather than letting them rule me. These small acts of surrender added up to a larger work of healing and freedom.

Making room for God isn't a one-time event; it's an ongoing process. Junk has to be cleared out regularly, and the Holy Spirit must have full access to every room in our lives. Are we willing to let Him in? To assess our "clutter" honestly and admit when something—be it a thought pattern, relationship, or habit—needs to go?

Let's not settle for being reluctant hosts. Let's invite the Holy Spirit to dwell in the hearts of our lives, not as a guest, but as the very foundation. Let's interact with Him, listen to His voice, and respond to His promptings. The more space we give Him, the more His presence can fill us, leading to the abundant life Jesus promises (John 10:10).

If we're willing to yield, He's willing to do the transforming.

True change doesn't come from forcing areas of your life into submission; it comes from trusting God and allowing Him to shape you into the person He wants you to be. When we take control of our lives and try to force outcomes, we're following another false guide—our own determination to be in charge. Like relying on our feelings, striving in self-sufficiency often leads us astray. We think we know what's good for us, but we really need the influence and perspective from the One who can truly lead and guide us.

Kilo

(to watch closely, observe, or examine)

1. Think about how you've handled stress in the past. Have you ever relied on something unhealthy?

2. Who or what has shaped your understanding of body image? Read Isaiah 64:8 and Jeremiah 18:1–6. What do these verses say about how God sees you?

3. Look over the "How to Tell if Something or Someone Controls You" list from this chapter. If any statements apply to you, take the first step toward breaking free and reach out to someone you trust for support.

4. Are there areas of your life you've kept "off-limits" to God?

5. Read John 12:20–25. What is one thing you need to surrender to God today?

Extra Resource

Stay rooted in Christ! Download a beautifully designed bookmark featuring a cacao pod growing close to the trunk—just like how we thrive when we stay connected to Jesus. Your bookmark will be a quiet reminder of a life-changing truth: fruit grows where there's connection. Just like that cacao pod depends on the tree for strength, nourishment, and support, we need Jesus for every step of our growth. We weren't designed to bear spiritual fruit through striving or self-effort but through staying close to Him.

Keep it in your Bible, journal, or planner as a quiet invitation to remain near Him, trust His guidance, and allow Him to do the growing. Its caption will remind you daily: "Spiritual fruit comes from being connected to Jesus."

Visit the following website to get your free bookmark or scan the QR code below.

https://www.fromhimnotthem.com/resources

7

Stressing ≠ Solving

"This is the last hardest thing we have to do, right?"
~ Lindsey R. Dennis

Mother's Day started out beautifully—almost perfect, even if my family had to be coaxed into a group photo. Little did I know that I wouldn't be smiling by the end of the day. After opening some sweet cards from my daughters, we went to church, where they gave each woman a rose along with some encouraging words. Later, we gathered with family for a meal.

After dinner with fresh strawberries for dessert (a May favorite in Maryland!), we took a walk around the farm. It was warm, and everything felt relaxed as we walked and chatted. Our daughters, niece, and nephew ran around us, laughing and playing, with my brother-in-law's dog, Charlie, dashing back and forth.

Charlie was a big, bouncy black Lab, only a puppy but already strong enough to knock someone over. Sometimes he ran so fast, we speculated he might have Greyhound blood. As we walked, Charlie ran circles around us, getting close but swerving away at the last second, like he was playing a game.

One moment, I was just walking—and the next, I was in the air! I hadn't seen the puppy coming. Charlie had run into me from behind, and before I knew it, I was airborne, feet up, hitting the ground with a thud. As I landed, the air rushed out of me, and pain spread through my whole body.

Dazed, I tried to get up. Trembling, I walked back to the farmhouse, each step painful. My body shook uncontrollably from the shock, and I felt strangely embarrassed. I wondered, *Is everyone looking at me? Are they judging me? Are they thinking I'm a wimp?*

Growing up, I hadn't spent much time around animals because some family members—myself included—were allergic to cats and dogs. I wasn't exactly an animal lover, and past run-ins with barking dogs had made me a little nervous around them. I was especially uneasy around Charlie, worried he'd jump on me or accidentally hurt me. And now, one of my fears had come true.

I blamed myself. Even though my family reassured me it was just an accident, I kept thinking, *I should have seen him coming. I should have moved aside.* I worried that everyone saw me as weak or overreacting. I worried that I was seriously injured. And I worried that my life might never get back to normal.

I don't remember consciously choosing that day to begin stressing, but that's what happened. Turning things over and over in my head became my new counterfeit guide to navigating this path I unexpectedly found myself on.

Initially, it made me feel like I was gaining some control over the situation, but all it did was take me further from peace. It was like following a GPS that keeps saying "recalculating" but never actually gets you to your destination. While it may have seemed like a logical reaction then, it ended up adding layers of stress and anxiety instead of clarity.

We've all had moments when we've thought, *I just can't deal right now.* Stressing feels like the only option, and we end up piling on guilt or self-blame, thinking we have to handle everything perfectly. But here's what we often miss in those moments: God's grace.

Stressing, however, is a counterfeit guide. It convinces us that we must carry the weight of our worries and expectations on our own, and that perfection is the only acceptable outcome. But this way of thinking leads us away from God, trapping us in a cycle of anxiety and exhaustion. Instead, God invites us to bring our cares to Him. When we're spiraling, overwhelmed by our own expectations or fears, God is there, offering His love and guidance. Stressing keeps us stuck, but trusting Him allows us to experience His grace in ways we never could on our own.

At fifteen, Ellie didn't know why life felt so hard. She could barely concentrate on her classes and her usual straight-A grades had dropped to D's and F's. Just getting up in the morning felt like a slog. She dreaded telling her parents about the dark thoughts crowding her mind, trying to convince her life wasn't worth living. She also found herself paralyzed by anxiety. When her mom asked her if she planned to go to the girls' small group at church, she made up excuses. *I'm too tired. Maybe next time. I'm not sure I like the leader.* But the truth was, the voice of anxiety was always screaming at her: "They'll think you're weird! They'll just reject you!"

Even though Ellie asked Jesus to take away the dark thoughts and give her peace, she felt like the storm inside of her was just getting worse. At youth group, a pastor had preached about focusing on serving others rather than ourselves, explaining that self-centeredness was like vanity. Another time, Ellie heard a pastor say that we just need more of God's Word and less of our feelings. These experiences didn't help—they made Ellie feel even more alone and confused as she wrestled with sadness and fear that wouldn't go away. She was too scared to tell anyone in her youth group about her struggles because she didn't want anyone to judge her.

Eventually, Ellie learned she had inherited a genetic predisposition toward mental health challenges from her parents and grandparents. She realized that caring for herself as God's beloved child was not selfish but necessary. With the help of a therapist and a psychiatrist, she began the arduous yet hopeful journey of recovery.[1]

In Christian circles, it can be even harder to admit to mental or physical struggles. We're often taught that poor health—especially of the mind—is a sign of weak faith. Illness is seen as the result of sin or spiritual failure: *You need to trust God more. Just pray about it. Go and walk in victory!*

If you've been part of a ministry where mental illness is acknowledged as a common struggle and people feel safe sharing about it, count yourself blessed. When I was a teen, mental illness was something people whispered about behind closed doors, often with furrowed brows and disapproving head shakes.

In many Christian circles, those who need more care than the average person—often labeled as "extra grace required" (EGR)—can feel like outliers, struggling to fit within the unspoken expectations of church culture. While pastoral care provides spiritual and relational support, most pastors are not equipped with the specialized training needed to address deep mental health struggles or trauma. Yet, there remains a longstanding expectation that pastors should be the primary caregivers, leading to pressure on both pastors and those in need. As a result, individuals who require more attention may feel ashamed for not "getting better" fast enough, while leaders may feel inadequate or overwhelmed.

Healthy, interdependent community reflects God's design, and sometimes, professional counseling—whether Christian or secular—plays a vital role in healing. Instead of seeing those with greater needs as burdensome or as people who "hog the air time" in group settings, we can shift our perspective to recognize their struggles with compassion and ensure they receive the right kind of care. All too often, we shame people for taking medication for anxiety or depression, assuming they're relying on a crutch rather than addressing the root of their struggles. But this judgment overlooks the fact that medication can be a legitimate tool to support healing and stability—not a sign of weakness or avoidance.

For too long, treating anxiety has been approached with a "just slap a Band-Aid on it!" mentality, focusing on quick fixes rather than addressing the deeper, underlying issues. Cover up your wound, forget about it, and it will heal. *Easy peasy.* We're supposed to effortlessly address our problems and move on. It's no wonder we struggle to give ourselves permission to *not* be okay.

If this has been your experience, I'm sorry. People often judge what they don't understand or fear. Sadly, putting someone else down can make us feel better about ourselves, convincing us we're not like them. But in doing so, we've also failed to recognize the value of support from outside the church—certified professionals with specialized training who can offer tools and strategies that promote real healing. Even if they don't share our faith, their expertise can still be a valuable resource, complementing the spiritual guidance we receive within the church.

When I listened to student struggles, my impulse was always to make it better right away! But I also had to face that I wasn't qualified to solve every problem. I could give spiritual help, but I wasn't a trained counselor or doctor. I had limits, and I couldn't solve everything.

My organization gave us a guide called "Stay in Your Lane: Our Role in Responding to Mental Health Issues." This was supposed to remind us of our roles and keep us from overstepping into areas where professional help was needed. But sometimes I worried. If a student was at risk of harming herself, I would wonder if being present could somehow stop her from doing so.

Over time, I learned about resources and where to send

students for the right help. Our team memorized the quickest route to the local hospital and knew where students could go for mental health support. I even had a counselor's number on speed dial. I learned my role wasn't to fix everything but to connect students to help while offering spiritual support. Yet, the urge to step in and "fix" things lingered.

When I faced health issues myself, I experienced my own version of these "lane issues." I wrestled with feeling that my recovery was up to me. When I struggled to heal, I found myself feeling shame. *Isn't counseling for crazy people? I should be able to figure this out. Maybe I'm not even a Christian because I'm not getting better.* I had to work through some of the same wrong beliefs about Christians and illness that Ellie did, especially the idea that I should be able to overcome everything easily with enough faith.

Here's the truth: Anxiety isn't something you just "stop" or "turn off." I'd heard people dismiss mental health struggles as something faith alone should correct, but I now understood it wasn't that simple. At times, it became unclear whether I was *choosing* to worry or if excessive ruminating/stressing was a result of my physical condition. I needed help, not judgment.

That realization shifted my perspective. For the first time, I saw that caring for my mind was just as important as caring for my body. Trusting God with my mental well-being became an essential part of trusting Him with my health as a whole.

Physical injury or illness can leave you with more questions than answers. Who do you turn to for help? What do you do when the advice you're given doesn't seem to work? It's overwhelming. Many of us are desperate to find clarity during our health struggles. When there aren't immediate answers, we can default to worrying—endless stressing over what may be wrong. But that constant anxiety can also reveal something deeper—how we often rely on our own strength instead of trusting God to guide us through times of uncertainty.

A painful bruise on my back was the visible reminder of my accident with Charlie. Although my ribs weren't broken, they were bruised, which meant I experienced pain every time I breathed, laughed, coughed, or sneezed. For four long months, taking deep breaths was painful. Breathing is something we take for granted, but imagine dreading every breath you take. I began to breathe shallowly, trying to avoid the pain.

Then came an even stranger symptom: *stridor*. This is when a person's breath makes a high-pitched noise because something is obstructing or narrowing their airway. The sound, like a screeching owl, could be heard at times when I tried to breathe in. Stridor made me feel like I wasn't getting enough air, and the fear of running out of breath kept me awake at night.

When I visited my family doctor for help, she suggested anti-anxiety medication to manage my symptoms. I appreciated the offer, but I left without filling the prescription. I didn't want to just mask my anxiety—I wanted a real solution. I thought, *If I can just get the right diagnosis, everything will be fine, and I'll be back to normal.*

But this wasn't just a passing worry—it had become a constant struggle. Instead of getting better, my worries kept building. *Why can't I fix this?* I kept asking myself. And the longer my health problems dragged on, the more anxious I felt. I wondered why God seemed to be delaying my healing. From morning to night, I was on edge.

Have you ever felt like you were walking around with a giant neon sign flashing above your head, declaring, "NOT OKAY"? That's how I felt as I battled my own struggles with mental health. For a long time, I tried to ignore the warning signs—pushing through, keeping busy, and pretending everything was fine. But the truth is, I wasn't fine.

It was in this state that the carefree philosophy of Timon and Pumbaa in *The Lion King* started to sound appealing. I wanted to sing "Hakuna Matata" right along with them. Their "it means no worries for the rest of your days" mindset felt like the escape I desperately needed. I longed for the days when life had felt simple and problem-free—when "no worries" were an achievable reality.

But life isn't a Disney movie. Problems and worries don't just disappear because we decide to ignore them or pretend they don't exist.

For the first time, I started experiencing panic attacks, which often hit me without warning. One even struck in the middle of a family outing to a themed dinner show, sending me to the bathroom, gasping for air as I tried to calm myself. I was supposed to be out cheering, enjoying the entertainment with my family—not hiding away, overwhelmed. When we left, I insisted Tim take me to urgent care, convinced something was majorly wrong with me.

Waiting in the clinic, I braced for bad news, but the nurse assured me my vitals were normal—I was breathing just fine. By then, the panic attack had subsided. I was relieved, but I hated constantly feeling torn between *okay* and *not okay*.

I grew up in a household where toughness was the default response. If I fell or got hurt, my dad's go-to advice was a cheerful "Walk it off!" Looking back, we can now laugh about it—Dad is a naturally positive person who always tries to focus on the bright side. But his tough-love approach sometimes had unintended consequences, like the time I kept playing through an All-Stars softball game after an injury. I ended up with a scar on my leg where I should have gotten stitches.

On a family trip to the beach, my dad, sister, and I were enjoying the ocean, jumping waves and body-surfing. Suddenly, a huge wave hit us, flipping me over so many times I couldn't tell which way was up. Back on shore, my sister held her left arm, crying and complaining that it hurt. Ever the optimist, my dad grabbed her arm, shook it, and encouraged, "You're fine, you're fine."

He wasn't trying to dismiss her pain—he just wanted to calm her down, the way we all do when we hope something isn't as bad as it seems. But as her pain didn't subside, my parents quickly had a lifeguard examine her arm. His advice? She needed to go to the hospital for an evaluation. Spoiler alert: She wasn't fine—her arm was broken!

Just like my dad hoped my sister's injury wasn't serious, we often try to convince ourselves that our own struggles aren't a big deal. When it comes to experiencing negative emotions, denial keeps us from addressing the root of the issue. Instead, we often turn to unhealthy coping mechanisms: substance abuse, overeating or undereating, binge-watching Netflix, or staying way too busy. Our culture encourages an "I'm fine" mentality, promoting escape through endless social media scrolling, constant activity, and anything that keeps us from being still and reflecting on what we're really feeling. We're convinced that "the good life" should be full of love, happiness, and joy. And as psychologist A. J. Adams points out, "we end up criticizing ourselves for feeling angry, anxious, or sad,"[2] which creates a cycle that can spiral into shame, guilt, or emotional avoidance.

So how do we break free from this cycle? How do we face the weight of our emotions without letting them consume us? The answer lies in bringing our struggles to God. He invites us to come to Him as we are, messy and broken, and He promises to carry our burdens. Jesus invites in Matthew 11:28–30, "Come to me, all who labor and are heavy laden, and I will give you rest. Take my yoke upon you, and learn from me, for I am gentle and lowly in heart, and you will find rest for your souls. For my yoke is easy, and my burden is light."

Learning to trust God with my mental health was a process. It didn't happen overnight. But as I began to bring my worries and struggles to Him, I found peace—not the absence of problems, but a deep sense of assurance that I wasn't walking through them alone. God was with me, giving me strength and guiding me step by step.

Because language changes over time, it's worth noting how modern psychologists and Scripture handle the concepts of worry and anxiety. Today, worry often seems harmless—just thinking or problem-solving about life's concerns.[3] *Should I have Chick-fil-A or Chipotle for dinner?* Often, we worry about more serious things, like paying for college. Worry becomes problematic, though, when it grows constant and consuming, veering into anxiety.[4]

Scripture also distinguishes levels of concern. Jesus addressed Martha when she was "anxious and troubled about many things" (Luke 10:41). Martha wasn't just concerned with a passing worry but by things that clouded her ability to see what mattered most. The phrase "many things" helps us see how Martha was overloaded. Many of us, like Martha, find ourselves burdened by multiple stressors, from work and school to responsibilities and relationships. Similarly, Proverbs 12:25 speaks to how "anxiety weighs down the heart" (niv). The implied heaviness of anxiety shows we can be hindered in our ability to function normally. Scripture is consistent in its teaching that we not allow worries to consume or control us. The distinction lies in how much space we allow worry to take up in our hearts and minds.

During my season of illness, I revisited Linda Dillow's *Calm My Anxious Heart*, especially her quote, "Worry is like a rocking chair; it will give you something to do, but it won't get you anywhere."[5] Solomon described this futility when he wrote, "Like clouds and wind without rain is a man who boasts of a gift he does not give" (Proverbs 25:14). Imagine the farmer eagerly watching the approaching clouds and wind, hoping his crops will receive a significant rainfall—only to be disappointed when no rain falls.

Anxiety is like that. It looks promising on the outside, but it turns out to be no gift at all.

In reality, anxiety doesn't keep us still, like a rocking chair—it pulls us in the wrong direction. The Hebrew word for anxiety, *merizo,* means "to distract" or "divide."[6] The "what ifs" of worry distract us, pulling our focus away from God.

Remarkably, Scripture also defines anxiety as "looking out for a thing"[7]—a way of striving to see, to control. I realized that by excessively worrying, I was trying to act as if I could control everything—*again*. But God, all-knowing and all-loving, asks me to give my concerns to Him instead. That's why Peter reminds us to "cast our cares on God" (1 Peter 5:7), and Jesus invites us to come to Him for rest.

There was one main question that nagged me throughout this season: *What do I have control over?* I wanted to obey Paul's command in Philippians 4:6 to be anxious for nothing, but I wondered if a biological component contributed to my anxious thoughts. If that was true, could I disregard Jesus' command not to worry about tomorrow (Matthew 6:34)? Did chemical imbalances beyond my control offer a "free pass" to anxiety?

Selena picked at her split ends to ease her stress. Her sisters yelled at her for it, but she didn't care. Anxiety wasn't something she chose—it just happened to her. She figured it was just part of her life now.

Then there was Zoe. Most days, she couldn't even find the energy to get out of bed. Everything her siblings did annoyed her. At night, as she drifted off to sleep, she thought, *Shame on me! If I were a better Christian, I wouldn't feel this way.*

While we might be tempted to respond to our struggles with a "Woe is me!" victim mentality like Selena or believe we deserve condemnation like Zoe, there's another approach. John describes Jesus as coming "from the Father, full of grace and truth" (John 1:14 niv). In this marriage of grace and truth lies healing. We can be gentle with ourselves, acknowledging that some of us are more susceptible to anxiety than others. Yet, as anxiety lies outside God's design, minimizing or ignoring it would mean overlooking a command to trust Him and not be troubled.

Ultimately, anxiety—whatever its origin—is a problem that needs addressing. It reflects both our fallen physical bodies and spiritual condition and therefore deserves attention on medical, psychological, and spiritual levels.

While seeking medical help to reduce anxiety, I determined to separate the fear-producing thoughts from my spiritual response to them. This is a practical outworking of a grace-and-truth response. We may not be able to stop the anxious thoughts themselves, but we can control our response. In faith, we can bring our cares to Jesus, trusting His promise of true rest. We can choose to seek holistic rest, believing that as we surrender our worries to Him, He will keep us unburdened by them. An anxiety-busting strategy using the acronym P.E.A.C.E. shows how we can do this:

- *P*ause and recognize the fear-inducing thought.
  Take a moment when an anxious or fear-inducing thought arises. Be honest about what's troubling you: *What if I fail this exam and ruin my future?*

- *E*valuate the thought without judgment.
  Accept the thought for what it is—just a thought, not an ultimate truth. Pay attention to where anxiety shows up in your body—maybe it's a tight chest or a headache. Your mind and body are connected, and recognizing this can help you release tension. Don't blame yourself for feeling anxious; instead, tell yourself, *I'm feeling anxious because*

this exam is important to me.

- ***A*pply God's truth to the thought.**
  Counter fear with Scripture, grounding yourself in God's promises and provision. God's Word says, "The heart of man plans his way, but the Lord establishes his steps" (Proverbs 16:9). This verse highlights that while we may make our own plans, God ultimately directs our future.

- **Cast your cares upon Jesus through prayer.**
  Surrender your specific worry to God: *Lord, I feel afraid that I'll fail, but I trust You to guide me. Help me to prepare well and give me peace in the process.*

- ***E*ngage in trust-filled action.**
  Do what you can while trusting God for the outcome. Surrender your tension to Him, both in body and mind. One simple way to do this is through Box Breathing—a practice you can use anytime, anywhere. To do this, sit or lie down in a comfortable position. Close your eyes and take a deep breath. Breathe in slowly for a count of four. Hold your breath for a count of four. Exhale slowly for a count of four. Hold your breath again for a count of four. Repeat this cycle for several minutes, or until you feel calmer.

  Then act responsibly: *I'll review my study material, take breaks, and remind myself that my worth isn't tied to my performance.*

The P.E.A.C.E. strategy will help you remember the anxiety-busting steps while also reinforcing the process of turning to God in moments of stress. When anxiety returns, you can repeat the process, reaffirming your trust in God.

Over time, my body healed, and I could finally draw full breaths again. While I still carry stress in my shoulders and neck, the stridor, panic attacks, and constant anxious thoughts gradually went away.

A turning point came when a friend suggested I support my adrenal glands—small organs above the kidneys that release hormones to manage stress. Mine were likely overtaxed from months of living in a constant, perceived emergency state. *Alert! Alert! Tracy needs more cortisol!* Within a month of daily taking herbal supplements, I felt noticeably less frazzled and depleted. Even now, a label that reads "support for the stressed and overworked" reminds me to prioritize my well-being.

While I personally found some relief through an adrenal supplement, I want to be clear that I am not a medical professional. Supplements and medications affect people differently, and what worked for me may not be right for you. Always consult a qualified healthcare provider before starting or changing any supplement or medication to ensure it's safe and appropriate for your individual needs.

Looking back, I can see some choices I'd make differently. I wouldn't have put all the pressure on myself to manage persistent anxious thoughts. For sure, I would have shared my struggles sooner. Talking to someone who had also dealt with anxiety helped normalize my experience and alleviated the shame I felt. I'd also have sought more help, not just from doctors but from trained mental health professionals too.

It's important to remember that God often works through other people to bring healing. You don't have to carry the burden alone. Reaching out to trusted friends, family members, a support group, or a therapist can be a huge step forward. Inviting others into your recovery process not only helps you feel less isolated but also allows them to offer wisdom, encouragement, and care when you need it most.

Seeking help from a secular professional can feel intimidating, but don't let that hold you back. If you can be a self-advocate and communicate clearly, you can ensure your faith and values are honored in the process. Be up front about what's important to you—let them know that praying to Jesus, not just meditation, is central to your healing and that you see things through the lens of the Bible. Some approaches may feel a little *woo woo*—overly mystical or tied to non-Christian spiritual practices—but certain techniques can be helpful when practiced in a way that aligns with biblical truth. The key is to approach everything with discernment, ensuring it points you toward God rather than away from Him.

If I had to do things over again, I'd extend myself more grace, giving myself permission to rest without guilt over falling behind in my roles as friend, mom, wife, or ministry worker. I'd remind myself that my worth isn't based on productivity, and I'd reject the lie that struggling with anxiety made me a weak Christian.

If anxiety is a regular part of your life, you're not alone. More of us struggle with it than we care to admit. Social psychologist Jonathan Haidt even calls those born after 1995 "the anxious generation." And pretending "we're fine" doesn't really help us move forward. If we want God to guide us, we need to learn to process our fears and emotions in a healthy way.

I know I'm struggling with anxiety when I wake up with a worry looping in my mind, or when I notice a tightness in my chest or an unsettled stomach. How about you? Can you recognize when anxiety has taken center stage in your life?

Here's the good news: We don't have to follow anxiety's lead. I've learned through experience that worrying may feel powerful and even convincing, but it's a poor guide. It can't offer clarity or peace—only more stress. However, when we take our anxieties to God, we make the choice to trust His guidance over the false promises of fear.

God's guidance offers something anxiety never can: stability in the storm and peace that surpasses understanding. By surrendering our worries to Him, we aren't just escaping anxiety; we're choosing to live with confidence, knowing the One who holds the future also holds us.

What if today, you took a small step toward trusting God with your anxiety? Maybe it's journaling your fears, praying honestly, or simply sitting quietly in His presence. These small, intentional choices add up, leading you away from the unproductive cycle of worry and into the peace God promises for those who trust Him. You're not in this alone—God's with you, ready to guide you through every season.

Kilo

(to watch closely, observe, or examine)

1. Have you ever feared your life wouldn't return to normal after a distressing event? Did you continue to worry—even long after the event was over—and find it hard to stay focused on finding a solution?

2. If you've faced mental health struggles, what advice have you received? Specifically, what guidance has your faith community encouraged or discouraged?

3. Read Matthew 6:25–34. What does Jesus tell us not to worry about?

4. How can you bring your worries to God? What practices help calm your fears (journaling, worshiping, reading Scripture, talking with a friend)? What steps could you take to seek help?

Extra Resource

The P.E.A.C.E. strategy is more than a helpful acronym—it's a tool you can return to again and again. Whether you're facing anxious thoughts, a stressful decision, or just need a moment to breathe, keeping these steps close can make all the difference. Also, you'll learn how to recognize stress showing up in your mind and body—and walk step-by-step toward calm and clarity. Download your printable version—something you can tuck in a notebook, tape to your mirror, or save to your phone. Let this simple reminder walk you back to peace when your thoughts start to spiral.

Visit the following website to download a printable PDF of this spiritual practice or scan the QR code below.

https://www.fromhimnotthem.com/resources

Download Here

8

Flirting with Spiritual Darkness

"Magic gives a person agency they wouldn't otherwise have, and I think that's particularly appealing to a child because children, inevitably, are quite powerless ... and the idea that you have secret power, extraordinary power, supernatural power, I think is hugely seductive to all of us."
~ J. K. Rowling

Are you a fan of epic adventures? If you love fantasy, you might have heard about *The Rings of Power*. It's a prequel to *The Lord of the Rings* and takes place thousands of years before the famous trilogy. One of the main characters, Galadriel, is not just the elegant and wise elf many fans know from the movies—she's also depicted as a fierce warrior.

In one episode, Galadriel is traveling with Theo, a boy who's been separated from his mom. As they hide from danger, Theo starts questioning the tough things in his life. He wonders how losing his home and maybe even his family could possibly be part of God's plan. Galadriel listens and then says, "I cannot see it yet."

Can you relate to that? Do you ever feel like you're stuck, unable to see how everything will work out? Maybe you're tired of making decisions, or life has thrown one problem after another at you. Or maybe you're just...bored. You wonder if there's something more to life—some purpose, some adventure, something ahead that will make all the struggle or waiting worth it.

We all want to see what's coming next, don't we? But what do we do when we can't see what's ahead, no matter how hard we try?

Sometimes, we try to take control in ways that don't work. We rely on our feelings to guide us, only to realize they aren't always right. We push and force things to happen, but it's exhausting. We stress and worry, hoping that will solve our problems, but it doesn't. And when none of that works, we flirt with darkness, turning to forbidden paths that promise answers—horoscopes, crystals, mediums, or rituals—without realizing how dangerous and deceptive they can be.

What if there's a better way?

The sleepover started out pretty normal. My twin sister and I had been invited, along with a few other seventh-grade girls, to spend the night at a friend's house. It was our first time there, so I felt nervous. But as we snacked and talked about which boys we liked, I began to relax.

Then someone suggested pulling out my friend's Ouija board. Immediately, I felt uncomfortable. My family didn't own this "game." If you've never seen one, a Ouija board is a flat board with letters, numbers, and symbols printed on it. Players place their fingers on a small piece of wood or plastic, which supposedly moves around the board to spell out messages. People use it to get answers or direction, like some kind of spiritual GPS.

I didn't know if my friends believed the board actually worked, or if they just thought it was fun and creepy. But even at thirteen, I knew it wasn't something I should mess with. The Bible warns us against trying to connect with spirits or seek supernatural guidance outside of God. I couldn't have told you the exact Bible verses, but I understood it was dangerous.

Why? Because there's real spiritual power involved—power that doesn't come from God. My friends didn't realize they were opening themselves up to something they couldn't control or trust. So, a couple of us who were Christians left the room while the others kept playing.

Why do people seek out knowledge of the future? Is it because we're resistant to change, hoping that a glimpse ahead will help us navigate transitions with more confidence? Or is it the allure of the unknown—the possibility that something greater, more exciting, or more fulfilling lies ahead? Perhaps it's a deep-seated desire for control, an attempt to prepare for the unpredictable so we don't feel powerless. Or maybe we've been fooled into believing that knowing the future will bring security, when in reality, it may only lead to more anxiety. At its core, the pursuit of the future often reveals something about our fears, our longings, and where we place our trust.

Do any of these statements sound familiar?

- *I'm afraid of what's ahead and want to know how to avoid trouble.*

- *I feel unsure about my choices and need someone or something to tell me what to do.*

- *I'm just curious and want to explore the unknown.*

Even though I stayed away from the Ouija board, I understand the desire to know what's next. Who doesn't want to feel more in control of their life? A sense of power comes with understanding—when we "see" or figure something out, it feels like we have the upper hand.[1] But when we turn to the wrong sources for that vision, like astrology or witchcraft, we risk being led down dangerous paths. These counterfeit guides might offer quick answers or a false sense of empowerment, but they quietly pull us away from God.

God wants us to live empowered lives, but not by attaching ourselves to things He didn't create for that purpose. When we seek direction, we need to turn to Him, the only trustworthy guide. Anything else can trap us, pulling us away from the freedom and security God provides.

The search for power and guidance isn't new. Throughout history, people have turned to outside sources for help. Ancient kings had their advisors—Egypt relied on magicians and sorcerers (Exodus 7:11), while Babylon used enchanters and astrologers (Daniel 2:27). These forbidden practices are part of what the Bible calls *divination*—trying to discover hidden knowledge through spiritual means (Leviticus 19:31).

But is it really so wrong to get a little "help"? If something could make your life better or change your future, wouldn't it be worth it?

When the Israelites were preparing to enter the Promised Land, God gave them a serious warning:

> When you enter the land the Lord your God is giving you, do not learn to imitate the detestable ways of the nations there. Let no one be found among you who sacrifices their son or daughter in the fire, who practices divination or sorcery, interprets omens, engages in witchcraft, or casts spells, or who is a medium or spiritist or who consults the dead. Anyone who does these things is detestable to the Lord; because of these same detestable practices the Lord your God will drive out those nations before you. You must be blameless before the Lord your God. (Deuteronomy 18:9–13 NIV)

Why was this such a big deal to God? Because turning to these practices is a form of idolatry—depending on something or someone other than God for security and guidance. It replaces trust in the Creator with trust in creation. Also, God wants to protect us from evil and the harm that engaging in these practices brings.

Margarita always felt drawn to the spiritual realm, even as a young girl. In her religious household, rules and behavior were emphasized more than a relationship with God, so she wasn't sure why she felt this pull to the spiritual world. Now, she recognizes that God is Spirit (John 4:24) and that connecting with Him happens spirit to spirit, but that wasn't always the case.

Initially, Margarita's journey left her feeling burned out and frustrated. She put much effort into praying, reading the Bible, and worshiping, hoping these actions would lead to the supernatural experience she craved. But instead of finding what she was looking for, she found exhaustion. What she didn't realize at the time was that she wasn't truly pursuing God for who He is; her deeper motivation was to have a spiritual encounter. When her efforts didn't produce the results she wanted, she became curious about what others were doing to access the spiritual realm.

Margarita noticed that many people, like her, wanted to explore both paths—the Christian and the mystical—because they were looking for guidance the church didn't always provide. Those involved in New Age practices—a spiritual movement that blends Eastern beliefs, mystical experiences, and self-empowerment—often seem to have the "spiritual" figured out, which makes it look so appealing to those who are searching for something deeper.

Here's the problem: New Age practices are a counterfeit of what God offers. And the thing about counterfeits is they're designed to look like the real thing. Think about a knockoff designer purse. At first glance, it seems like the real deal. Without closer inspection, it's hard to tell the difference. That's why spiritual counterfeits are so tempting. They seem accessible, promise power, and come with rituals that seem to deliver results. In the short-term, it "works."

Counterfeits often try to "one-up" the real thing. It's like the playful rivalry in the song "Anything You Can Do" from *Annie Get Your Gun,* where one person insists they can outdo the other at everything. The back-and-forth boasts—claiming to be stronger, faster, and better in every way—mirror how spiritual counterfeits try to imitate and surpass the real power and truth found in God.

But when it comes to the spiritual realm, nothing can one-up the kingdom of God. The kingdom of heaven is far greater than anything the kingdom of darkness can offer.

Through observing New Age practices and asking her friends many questions, Margarita discovered that the dark side teaches that everyone is a divine being. The spiritual journey is about gaining more power by reaching a higher state of being. But this path often requires actions that feel uncomfortable, and the deeper you go, the more it leads to the occult—hidden spiritual practices that seek supernatural power apart from God. The only promise it offers is power, but over time, it leaves you feeling isolated, lonely, depressed, and angry.

Engaging with the spiritual realm outside of God's kingdom opens the door for Satan to gain influence in your life. But who is Satan? Satan is a created being who once held a position of great beauty and power in heaven. However, his pride led him to rebel against God, and he was cast out (Isaiah 14:12–15; Revelation 12:7-9). Now, he works to deceive and oppose God's purposes, prowling like a roaring lion, seeking to lead people away from God (1 Peter 5:8; 2 Corinthians 11:14). While Satan's goal is to steal, destroy, and keep you from the life God intends, God's invitation is the complete opposite. He calls you to draw near to Him, where you'll find family, community, love, peace, joy, freedom, and your true identity.

Everything changed when Margarita stopped observing New Age practices and engaging in religious striving. Instead of trying to force her way into the spiritual realm, she simply rested in God's love. By focusing on her relationship with Him—not *chasing experiences*—she discovered that God helped her spiritually connect with Him in deeply satisfying ways.

Margarita decided to let go of her agenda and asked herself if she truly wanted to know God for who He is, not just for what He could give her. She began to pursue a deeper relationship with the Father, spending time with Him and seeking His heart. In doing so, she found rest for her soul, stability, and a greater understanding of her identity as someone deeply loved and cared for by God. Trusting Him with the desires of her heart, Margarita experienced both the joy and sorrow of seeing others through His eyes, feeling His love for them in a powerful way. She also received insights from the Holy Spirit about other people—insights she could never have known on her own—which allowed her to encourage them in ways that were deeply personal and impactful.

The truth is, everyone has access to the spiritual realm. Margarita likes to say that you can enter through alignment with God's kingdom or through rebellion against it. For those in Christ, the Spirit dwells within us, and we have authority over spiritual powers through Him. But without Christ, people turn to other channels—like New Age practices—to connect with the spiritual. And the deeper someone goes into these practices, the more they pay the price.

Margarita observed this firsthand. Many of her friends involved in New Age practices experienced constant inner chaos and unrest. One time, Margarita was sharing a hotel room with a friend for several nights. Each evening, her friend carefully arranged crystals and figurines on her bed and around the room, hoping they would bring protection and help her sleep better. One afternoon, while her friend was out, Margarita prayed earnestly for her friend, asking God to bring freedom and peace. She trusted in the power of Jesus to overcome darkness and bring truth (Colossians 1:13, 1 John 4:4). The next morning, her friend remarked that she'd had the best night's sleep in as long as she could remember. In fact, she was so tired that she didn't do the new moon ceremony she'd planned.

The more involved Margarita's friends got in New Age spiritual practices, the more it demanded of them. Some ceremonies or meditation practices brought them face-to-face with terrifying entities and oppressive darkness.

There are two very different paths to spiritual encounters: one through a relationship with God and the other through practices associated with darkness. The path you choose matters. God created you for a relationship with Him. When you pursue Him for who He is—seeking His heart and desiring to know Him—any spiritual encounters you have will be the natural result of that relationship. Don't settle for chasing experiences that promise quick answers or excitement but ultimately leave you empty. Instead, focus on drawing close to God, trusting Him to reveal Himself in His perfect timing and in ways that are good for you. Let your encounters with the supernatural be a byproduct of a life centered on Him.

Now, let's get back to the story of Israel. Unfortunately, the Israelites did not remain guiltless. Despite repeated warnings from God's messengers about the dangers of seeking the occult for guidance, they succumbed to temptation.[2] Attempting to unlock the secrets of the future—whether for political, financial, or personal gain—was an apple they couldn't resist.

One vivid example is found during Saul's reign as king. When the Philistines attacked, Saul was terrified and sought advice from God. But because Saul had repeatedly disobeyed the Lord, including failing to follow instructions during the battle with Amalek, God was silent. Instead of repenting and waiting on the Lord, Saul disguised himself and sought guidance from a medium (1 Samuel 28).

Saul's reasoning might feel familiar: *I have to do something. God isn't answering, so I'll figure it out myself. It's just this once—what could it hurt?*

The harm, however, is significant. Satan masquerades as an angel of light, and his servants disguise themselves as messengers of righteousness. They promise freedom but bring bondage. When we open ourselves to guidance from sources other than God, we invite spiritual deception and demonic persuasion into our lives. The enemy, called the father of lies (John 8:44), uses subtle means to make his influence seem harmless, even helpful.

Satan's messengers suggest you need a bridge to heavenly realms. They dismiss the sufficiency of Jesus, who already bridged the separation between us and the Father. Instead, they offer their services. Psychic mediums and fortune-tellers claim to unlock your potential, guide your destiny, and heal your spirit.

For skeptics, the appeal might be subtler. Driving home one day, I noticed a sign on a nearby building advertising crystals and energy healing. For seventy dollars a month, you could book a session to "balance your energy." Or you could buy a crystal, retreat to a dark room, meditate, and let the crystal guide your decisions. These practices promise clarity and healing, but they subtly replace God's role as our source of wisdom and peace.

Belief in spiritual intermediaries is not a new phenomenon. Some ancient Hawaiians, for example, believed in *aumakuas,* ancestral spirits thought to inhabit animals like sharks or owls. These spirits were believed to offer protection, guidance, and blessings like charisma or intelligence.[3] My Native Hawaiian friend Hālina explains this practice as a misuse of God's creation—a way of relating to animals that was never part of His original design.

This blending of spiritual beliefs is a form of *syncretism*, a danger Christians have faced for centuries. In his book *The Shark God,* Charles Montgomery describes how missionaries in the South Pacific encountered dark magic interwoven with Christian teachings.[4] Even in Hawai'i's Great Awakening of the 1800s—where thousands came to Christ—syncretism crept in. The revival was diluted and people were pulled away from pure devotion to Jesus.[5]

Today, we face similar challenges. Like shoppers visiting multiple stores to find the best deals, we may look to Jesus *and* other sources for guidance and empowerment. But this approach undermines our trust in God, who is meant to be our sole source of wisdom and strength.

If you encounter something that makes you hesitate or question its spiritual validity, take action. Don't ignore the *Hmmm...* moments. Turn to Scripture, seek counsel from trusted believers, and invite God into the conversation. James assures us: "If any of you lacks wisdom, let him ask God, who gives generously to all without reproach, and it will be given him" (1:5).

God's guidance is never out of reach for those who sincerely seek Him.

Many of us have grown up experiencing lighter takes on a darker supernatural world. We've screamed at ghost stories, watched horror movies through our fingers, and dressed up for trick-or-treating on Halloween. And who hasn't braved a haunted hayride as a rite of passage? Best case: You have fun, get a little spooked, and laugh with your friends. Worst case: You're up all night, haunted by nightmares of a chainsaw-wielding maniac.

Many of us treat the supernatural world like a harmless thrill, but is it really? Those Magic 8 Balls ("Will I pass my math test?")

Shake-shake-shake... "Ask again later..."), palm-reading booths at carnivals, and playful nods to the occult may seem like innocent fun, but they can desensitize us to a deeper, more dangerous reality.

Scripture doesn't take such things lightly. Whenever God's people engaged in occult practices, it's described as evil in His sight. These actions provoked God to anger and led to serious consequences. Saul, Israel's first king, provides a sobering example. When he turned to a medium for guidance instead of seeking the Lord, his disobedience sealed his fate: "He broke faith with the Lord in that he did not keep the command of the Lord, and also consulted a medium, seeking guidance. *He did not seek guidance from the Lord*. Therefore, the Lord put him to death and turned the kingdom over to David the son of Jesse" (1 Chronicles 10:13–14, emphasis mine).

God often allows people to pursue what they want, even when it's harmful. Because Israel rejected Him, God withdrew His presence, leaving them vulnerable to exile. Similarly, when we turn to occult practices, we risk driving away God's presence in our lives.

Do you know what the problem with flirting is? *You never know who you're going to attract.* And sometimes, the people we attract won't leave us alone, even when we're no longer interested in a relationship. When we flirt with forbidden spiritual channels, we risk inviting dangerous spiritual beings into our lives. We need Jesus to break us free from our entanglement with hidden powers.

Mark had a deeply unsettling experience during an ayahuasca ceremony—a ritual involving a powerful hallucinogenic brew—where he was confronted by death and experienced hell. Afterward, he began searching for meaning. During a rebirthing healing session, he was led to visualize a door by the healing facilitator. When he opened it, he witnessed the presence of Jesus Christ behind it. Mark sensed that Jesus was the answer, while the other path seemed tied to the darkness he'd encountered in the ceremony.

Some time later, Mark's faith was tested in a moment of crisis. In preparation for the home birth of his daughter, he had arranged crystals and performed rituals beforehand, hoping for a good outcome. But when his daughter was born, she wasn't breathing and seemed lifeless. The creepy and distressing feeling from his ayahuasca ceremony resurfaced. So, Mark turned to a cross nearby that his family had given him when he was a child. Gripping the cross, he prayed and asked Jesus for help. Moments later, his daughter began to breathe. This experience provided Mark and his family with the conviction to leave all other spiritual paths behind and put their faith in Jesus Christ.

In Jesus' time, people also turned to witchcraft and sorcery for answers. The book of Acts records several instances where magic practitioners were called out (8:9, 13:6). However, something remarkable happened when people put their trust in Jesus: They abandoned these practices entirely.

Also many of those who were now believers came, confessing and divulging their practices. And a number of those who had practiced magic arts brought their books together and burned them in the sight of all. And they counted the value of them and found it came to fifty thousand pieces of silver. So the word of the Lord continued to increase and prevail mightily (Acts 19:18–20).

This significant financial loss illustrates how highly these books were valued. Yet, the new believers willingly gave them up, recognizing that trust in anything apart from God was ultimately worthless.

My friend Natalie grew up fascinated by stories about witches and vampires. Coming from a tough home life, she was drawn to anything that made her feel more in control. As she got older, social media introduced her to practices like "kitchen witchcraft"—using spells and rituals while cooking.

It didn't seem like a big deal. Natalie was raised Catholic, so when she came across something called "Christian Witchcraft," it didn't sound too strange. The idea was to honor Christ as a spiritual master while doing spells for love or good purposes. She thought she could use her "powers" to help others and even make life better for herself.

She started taking classes from a high Wiccan priestess—Wicca being a modern pagan, nature-based religion that involves rituals, spellwork, and reverence for various deities. She bought a wand, candles, crystals, and a book for casting spells. Natalie learned how to make perfumes, set up altars, and even talk to "spirit guides." For ten years, she relied on these practices to feel enlightened and powerful.

But one day, God stepped in. While listening to a Christian speaker online, Natalie felt God saying to her that she didn't really know Him. That moment shook her. She realized her efforts to control her life had led her away from God, not toward Him.

Over the next year, Natalie began studying the Bible. She joined a church where pastors helped her renounce her pagan practices. She got rid of her spell books, perfumes, and other tools of witchcraft. Most importantly, Natalie surrendered her life to Jesus and began a real relationship with Him. Through the Holy Spirit, she found the peace and purpose she had been searching for all along.

Maybe you've never been involved in witchcraft like Natalie, but I'm sure you've been tempted to look for guidance or control outside of God. Perhaps you've checked your daily horoscope for insight, tried manifesting a specific outcome, or put your faith in lucky charms. Maybe you've consulted tarot cards or followed moon phases for timing rituals. But those paths will only leave us empty and far from Him. Whatever we trust, follow, or depend on shapes us. The Bible warns that when Israel followed worthless idols, they became worthless themselves (2 Kings 17:15). The same is true today.

What are you trusting for guidance, direction, or confidence? Are you relying on things that reflect God's truth, or are they pulling you away from Him? It's easy to be deceived by things that feel harmless or even helpful. But true guidance and lasting value come from God alone.

Instead of feeling or forcing your way through life, worrying constantly, or flirting with spiritual darkness, we can trust God to lead us. When we focus on Him, He fills us with His Spirit and equips us to walk in truth and freedom. We escape from the spiritual bondage these other guides provide, and we experience the security of knowing that someone who truly loves and cares for us will not lead us astray. Paul encourages, "If God is for us, who can be against us? He who did not spare his own Son but gave him up for us all, how will he not also with him graciously give us all things?" (Romans 8:31-32).

Kilo

(to watch closely, observe, or examine)

1. What are you looking for? Why do you sometimes want help seeing the future? Read Proverbs 2:6–15. What does God promise to give you instead?

2. What do you trust? What things—like fame, money, power, or nature—might you put your confidence in instead of God? Check your phone's screen time. Does it show anything you might need to change?

3. What choices are you making? Read Deuteronomy 30:11–20 about choosing life or death. How have your choices reflected life with God or life apart from Him?

4. Is there anything you need to let go of? Read Acts

19:18–20. Ask God to show you if there's anything in your life that doesn't honor Him, especially spiritual practices. If so, ask for help from a trusted friend, pastor, campus ministry leader, or therapist to let go and walk in freedom.

Extra Resource

Satan doesn't just lure people with the obvious traps—sometimes, his most dangerous lies sound almost true, especially in religious spaces. The "5 Lies Holding You Back—And The Truth That Sets You Free" will help you recognize and reject the subtle deceptions that can weaken your faith and keep you from walking in God's truth. Don't let these lies hold you back—arm yourself with the truth that sets you free!

Visit the following website to download this Truth & Lies Cheat Sheet or scan the QR code below.

https://www.fromhimnotthem.com/resources

PART THREE
GETTING TO KNOW
THE HOLY SPIRIT

9

Carrying the Spirit with Confidence

**"... but you shall cling to the Lord your God
just as you have done to this day."
Joshua 23:8**

Growing up, my family had strong football loyalties. Sundays meant church in the morning and sports the rest of the day. We cheered loudly for the Pittsburgh Steelers and Penn State, except for my brother, the family's black sheep—he roots for Michigan. While football games kept me on the edge of my seat, the low whispers of golf commentary often lulled me to sleep.

Football, though, is a thrill to watch. Have you ever seen a quarterback get sacked? That's when the defense breaks through and tackles him before he can throw the ball. Sometimes, he never sees it coming.

What about you? Have you ever been "sacked" by life?

Maybe something caught you off guard—unexpected heartache, a failure, or a situation you weren't prepared to handle. Maya didn't expect the loneliness that hit when she left for college. Naomi, searching for approval and love, lost herself in the party scene. Amy's world shifted when she faced an unexpected pregnancy.

You might feel crushed, like you can't get back up. Perhaps you've watched others succeed while you're still waiting for your turn, or the rejection from your dream college still stings. Perhaps you're carrying something even heavier—the pain of your parents getting divorced, the alienation of your friend group dropping you, the loss of someone you love, or the deep wounds of sexual assault.

Life can hit hard. And when it does, big questions can flood our minds: *Is God really good? Why does He let bad things happen? Where is He when I'm hurting?*[1]

These aren't easy questions to answer. And sometimes, even after wrestling with God and Scripture, the answers we find still don't satisfy us—and we're even more confused than ever.

But here's the good news: God sees you, even in your hardest moments. He cares about you and your journey. And He doesn't leave you to figure it out alone.

God gave His best gift—Jesus. Jesus willingly took the ultimate "sack" when He died on the cross, taking the punishment for our sins. But He didn't stop there. Before His death, Jesus made a promise to His disciples: "I will ask the Father, and he will give you another Helper, to be with you forever... He dwells with you and will be in you" (John 14:16–17). That Helper is the Holy Spirit, sent to guide us, strengthen us, and help us through life.

Here's the deal, though: You can't have one without the other. If you want the Spirit's help, you need Jesus too. Think of it like a "BOGO: Buy One, Get One" sale. Sometimes, stores make you buy two items to get the deal. Even if you think you only need one, they come as a pair. That's how it is with Jesus and the Spirit—they're a package deal! You might not realize it yet, but you need both Jesus and the Spirit to live the thriving life God desires for you.

When life knocks you down, don't try to get up by focusing on your feelings, forcing your way forward, being anxious about what else might go wrong, or looking for someone to assist you who isn't safe. Instead, follow the lead of the Holy Spirit. He's here to help—because God isn't just watching from the sidelines. He's with you, every step of the way.

Like many of you, I love playing sports. The fun of competition and the joy of working with a team has taught me valuable lessons: the importance of practice, perseverance, dedication, and even how to deal with disappointment. Sports are more than just games—they're a way to experience the highs and lows of life in a safe space.[2]

In fact, the New Testament writers often used athletic examples, like running and boxing, to help Christians grow spiritually. I sometimes wonder if football would have made the list if it had been around back then!

Now, for those of you who don't care much for football—maybe it's just something your parents, siblings, or friends obsess over—don't worry! I promise not to overwhelm you with football talk. I'll use just enough examples to make my points clear, and who knows? You might even impress someone with your football knowledge after this (or be prepared for the next Taylor Swift Super Bowl). But more importantly, these illustrations will help you see the Holy Spirit in a fresh, exciting way.

Think of me as your spiritual trainer. I've spent over thirty years walking with Jesus and learning to rely on the Holy Spirit. I'm still learning, but I want to share what I've discovered to help you grow too. The tips in this book are starting points, meant to guide and inspire you. As you grow in your relationship with the Holy Spirit, you'll discover even more about His work in your life.

As we start our training, we need to cover something foundational.

The Holy Spirit is everything.

To understand this, let's start with the actual football. The ball itself is everything in the game. The quarterback can't score without it. Every play, every moment of the game, revolves around who controls the ball. Because the quarterback starts every play with control of the ball, he's the most important and powerful player on the field.

In a similar way, the Holy Spirit is essential in our lives. He's not optional if we want to live with purpose, power, and influence. The Holy Spirit enables us to experience God working in and through us, and He equips us to impact the lives of others. But just like the quarterback must take the ball with him, we need to carry the Holy Spirit with us and follow His lead.

In the Old Testament, the Holy Spirit's work was temporary and task-specific.[3] God empowered certain people for specific purposes, but His presence wasn't permanent. Writers used a variety of verbs to describe this empowering: "to rest or fall on, to take hold of, to lift up, to bring here or there, to enter into, to fill, and to invest."[4]

But under the new covenant Jesus inaugurated, everything changed. The Holy Spirit now permanently dwells within every believer. When you trust in Jesus' life, death, and resurrection, you receive eternal life—and the gift of the Holy Spirit: And Peter said to them, "Repent and be baptized every one of you in the name of Jesus Christ for the forgiveness of your sins, and you will receive the gift of the Holy Spirit. For the promise is for you and for your children and for all who are far off, everyone whom the Lord our God calls to himself" (Acts 2:38–39).

No one has exclusive access to the Spirit—not the most famous Christian you can think of, not missionaries, not your small group or campus ministry leader. The same Spirit who empowers them lives in you. Let it sink in: *You are a dwelling place for God, a place where His presence moves in and through your everyday life.* Just as the Israelites once visited the tabernacle to encounter God's presence, His Spirit now resides in you, permanently.

In Old Testament times, access to God was limited. Ordinary people came and went from the tabernacle, while select priests served in the holy places. Only the high priest, after purifying himself, could enter the "Most Holy Place" once a year to offer a blood sacrifice for Israel's sins. This sacrifice restored fellowship with God—but only temporarily (Hebrews 9:7).

My friend and theological director, Byron Straughn, once compared these Old Testament sacrifices to paying with a credit card. When you buy something with your card, the transaction is approved, but the actual payment isn't made until you pay the bill from your bank account.

Jesus, our great High Priest, fully paid the "bill" with His blood. His sacrifice was perfect and final, offering complete forgiveness of sins (Hebrews 9:11–12). Just as a paid credit card bill can't be charged again, your sin debt has been canceled—forever!

Because of Jesus, we now have direct access to God. We don't need an intermediary to pray, understand Scripture, or serve Him. The Holy Spirit empowers us to do all these things—and more.

We also take on roles that once belonged to Old Testament priests and prophets. As Spirit-filled believers, we're called to be witnesses, sharing and shining God's light into the world's darkness: "You are the light of the world. A city set on a hill cannot be hidden. Nor do people light a lamp and put it under a basket, but on a stand, and it gives light to all in the house. In the same way, let your light shine before others, so that they may see your good works and give glory to your Father who is in heaven" (Matthew 5:14–16).

My mom used to brightly encourage, "Shine for Jesus today!" as she dropped me off at school. While back then I rolled my eyes at her words, I've now caught the vision behind them as an adult. The truth remains: *We're called to reflect Christ's light in a dark world.*

The apostle Peter beautifully describes our identity and purpose:

> But you are a chosen race, *a royal priesthood,* a holy nation, a people for his own possession, *that you may proclaim the excellencies of him who called you out of darkness into his marvelous light.* Once you were not a people, but now you are God's people; once you had not received mercy, but now you have received mercy. (1 Peter 2:9–10, emphasis mine)

As believers, we've become God's temple—the meeting place where His Spirit dwells. The roles of priest and prophet, once limited to a select few, are now entrusted to every Spirit-filled Christian. Not only does the Spirit work in us, but He also works through us to accomplish God's purposes. We have the privilege of partnering with the Holy Spirit to bring light and hope to others.

Over my years of ministry, I've noticed that the Holy Spirit is the least understood person of our triune God. Some students think of Him as a ghost, a vague energy, or something mysterious and distant. When I ask students what they know about Him, I often get blank stares or nervous pauses.

That's why I created this list to help you further see some of the incredible ways the Holy Spirit works.

Top 10 Things the Holy Spirit Does

1. **Speaks what He hears from the Father and the Son**, with whom He is coequal and   coeternal (John 16:13).

2. **Guides us into truth** (v. 13).

3. **Reveals what is to come** (John 16:14).

4. **Understands the thoughts of God** and helps us understand salvation and life (1 Corinthians 2:11–12).

5. **Comforts us** in times of need (John 14:26).

6. **Empowers us** to be witnesses for God (Acts 1:8).

7. **Prays for us** when we don't know what to pray (Romans 8:26).

8. **Sets us apart** to live holy lives (1 Peter 1:2).

9. **Seals us** as God's own and assures us we belong to Him (2 Corinthians 1:22).

10. **Guarantees our inheritance** in God's kingdom (2 Corinthians 5:5, Ephesians 1:13).

This is just the tip of the iceberg when it comes to the Holy Spirit's work! I encourage you to read these New Testament verses and the context of their surrounding passages to gain a fuller understanding of what the Holy Spirit can do in your life.

When you understand how vital the Spirit's work is in your life, you'll make statements like these:

"I have a new understanding that I have the Holy Spirit in me 24/7, and I am excited to access Him and live with more fruit of the Spirit everywhere I go." (Ariana, 19)

"I cannot force myself to produce the fruits of the Spirit—I need to be more dependent on Him and allow Him to lead." (Alexis, 16)

"I can literally do NOTHING without the Holy Spirit. I HAVE to abide in Him." (Makayla, 18)

"I need to humble myself and let the Spirit work in me." (Sierra, 20)

"I learned about the hardship of growth and how to live by the strength of the Holy Spirit. I want to intentionally make more time with God." (Jade, 17)

Now that we've covered some basics and we understand why the Holy Spirit is everything, we're ready for another training tip!

In football, ball security is fundamental. Players train relentlessly to catch the ball, hold it tight, and protect it from their opponents. With practice, they learn to carry it close to their bodies, minimizing the risk of fumbles.

A football player can't do anything without possessing the ball. If he doesn't catch a pass, the play stops. In the same way, if life were a game, trying to play it without the Holy Spirit would be pointless. *As Christians, we need to establish Holy Spirit security—because without it, we'll find ourselves struggling.*

Julie accepted Christ when she was young, yet she couldn't understand why lying had such a hold on her. No matter how many times she told herself to stop, the habit remained. Then there's Tina, who constantly found herself using foul language, especially under stress. Nicole, a new believer, carried deep hatred toward her stepdad, unable to let go of the bitterness despite knowing God wanted her to.

Each of these young women genuinely desired to change, but they felt powerless to do so. Whether it's inward attitudes or outward behaviors, we will only find frustration and disappointment if we try to grow in Christ on our own and without the help of the Holy Spirit.

But here's the good news: Just as a football is passed to a player, the Holy Spirit has been given to us. We don't have to seize Him by our own effort—He is already ours. Here's how we secure Him: Picture a gift someone gave you recently—maybe for Christmas or your birthday. What did you do to make it yours? (Don't overthink it; it's not a trick question!) You had to *receive* it. A gift sitting unopened on a table is technically yours, but not truly yours—not in the full sense of the word.

Have you ever had a gift that remained unused? Maybe it's still in its original packaging or tucked away in a closet. Sometimes, we underestimate a gift's value. We assume we won't need it, misunderstand its purpose, or question the giver's intentions.

Imagine unwrapping a beautiful new sweater only to think, *The person who gave me this gift must not like my style.* Or opening an oversized laundry bin and wondering, *Is this a not-so-subtle hint about my cleaning habits?* When we misinterpret the heart of the giver, we miss the joy the gift was meant to bring.

Thankfully, God's Word makes His intentions clear when it comes to the gift of the Holy Spirit: He gave Him to us as a blessing. Setting the mind on the Spirit brings life and peace (Romans 8:6), and doing life with the Spirit ensures we have someone to help us in our weakness (v. 26).

When we fail to embrace the Spirit fully, we're like someone ignoring the value of a revolutionary gift. Take an Instant Pot, for example. These multifunctional kitchen devices can replace slow cookers, rice cookers, and sauté pans. Yet, I've had conversations with loved ones who resist even trying an Instant Pot. They're used to what they have and don't want to learn something new.

But talk to those who have made the switch, and you'll hear rave reviews: *This has changed my life! I can't believe I ever managed without it! I'll never go back to cooking the way I did before!*

It's the same with the Holy Spirit. Some Christians, while technically possessing the Spirit, haven't yet fully embraced Him. They rely on familiar but ineffective substitutes—like feelings, force, or frantic effort—to navigate life. But when you begin living in step with the Spirit, you'll look back and say, *I didn't know what I was missing!*

Receiving the Holy Spirit is like accepting a gift: You reach out, unwrap it, and begin to use it. In spiritual terms, this happens through prayer—talking with God. Before I share a prayer to help you secure the Spirit, I want you to understand that we're commanded to "be filled with the Holy Spirit" (Ephesians 5:18b). Why is this command necessary? Because it's not intuitive. Just as I remind my kids to clean their rooms or finish their homework, God instructs us to do things we wouldn't naturally do on our own. Without the instruction to zero in on being filled with the Spirit, we end up navigating life on our own, relying on the wrong guides.

Yet, God has equipped us to obey His commands, and when we ask Him to fill us with His Spirit, we can be confident He will answer: "And this is the confidence that we have toward him, that if we ask anything according to his will he hears us. And if we know that he hears us in whatever we ask, we know that we have the requests that we have asked of him" (1 John 5:14–15). Because being filled with the Spirit is God's will, we can trust He will grant this request.

When we're filled with the Spirit, the impossible becomes possible. Jasmine and her boyfriend stopped having sex after inviting the Spirit to guide their relationship in a way that honored God. Lavinia found the strength to forgive her friend, who had betrayed her trust by sharing something private. And Leilani overcame her shyness to boldly tell her classmate she was a Christian and offer to pray for her friend's struggles.

Your experience of being filled with the Holy Spirit may vary. Some people feel peace, joy, or a tangible sense of God's presence. Others cry, laugh, or even receive a spiritual gift (1 Corinthians 12:4–11). Keira felt an overwhelming wave of relief when she invited the Spirit to be active in her life. No longer did she feel like she had to become more Christ-like on her own; she felt hope rise as the Spirit's supernatural power became available to her. Ophelia, after asking the Spirit to fill and empower her, was unexpectedly overcome with joyous laughter, a sense of wholeness filling her being. Jennie, too, experienced the Spirit's work as she discerned God was preparing her to teach and explain the Bible in ways that would help others understand and apply it. She didn't hear an audible voice but had a clear sense of direction for her future.

Even if you don't feel anything, don't let that discourage you. God's promises are not dependent on feelings. By faith, believe that you have been filled with the Spirit and now have full access to Him. It's important to remember this because there will be times when you pray and *don't feel any different*. Let me assure you, it's not because the prayer didn't work. In fact, those times when you don't sense any change are when you need to exercise your faith. Believe that you are truly filled and empowered no matter whether you feel different or not.

If you're ready to receive the Holy Spirit—or renew your connection with Him—here's a prayer to guide you.

Heavenly Father, Thank You for the gift of the Holy Spirit. I admit that I've doubted His work in my life, and I've often thought I can navigate life on my own. Forgive me for believing the lie that Your Spirit is optional. I need You, Holy Spirit! By faith, I receive You into my life. Fill me with Your presence and power. Work in me and through me for Your glory. Help me to live each day in step with You. Amen.

With hours of practice, a player builds the confidence to perform under pressure on game day. This training includes running plays, strength conditioning, and studying the opponent's tactics. The goal is to handle the football so much that moving it down the field feels natural, leading to a touchdown.

Just as a player trains to perform under pressure on game day, we need to prepare for life's challenges by deepening our relationship with the Holy Spirit. *The more we focus on Him, communicate with Him, and rely on His guidance, the more naturally we'll live a Spirit-directed life, ready to face whatever comes our way.* It's game-day confidence applied to our real lives.

Here's one last illustration to help us understand this dynamic relationship and how to further secure the Spirit and His energizing power. Imagine chocolate milk.[5] Yep, no football this time, just a tall, refreshing glass of ice-cold chocolate milk.

When I was young, I made my own chocolate milk because the pre-made version was expensive (and less fun). Start with a tall glass of cold milk. Add a generous squeeze of chocolate syrup—Hershey's if you have good taste! Is it chocolate milk yet? No.

What transforms the milk into chocolate milk? You have to stir it. Until you do, the chocolate syrup settles at the bottom, separate from the milk. An unmixed glass tastes like milk, not chocolate—even though the milk contains the chocolate syrup.

This simple illustration mirrors the Holy Spirit's function in our lives. When we trust in Christ, the Spirit comes to live in us, much like adding chocolate syrup to milk. But without stirring or activating the Spirit, the Spirit's influence can settle. If we neglect our connection, the Spirit is present but not actively working through us. Our lives don't reflect the Spirit's influence, much like the glass of milk that needs a vigorous stirring.

The act of stirring—maintaining intimacy with the Spirit—requires intentionality. It's a continual process, especially when sin disrupts our relationship (more on that in the next chapter).

My goal each morning is to "stir" the Spirit by engaging with Him through:

- **Conversation** – I talk to Him freely, sharing my concerns for the day.

- **Invitation** – I ask Him to empower and guide me.

- **Listening** – I try to be still and hear His voice.

- **Confession** – When the Spirit reveals sin, I acknowledge and address it.

I also pray a version of this prayer.

> *Holy Spirit, thank You that You want to have relationship with me and that You want to draw me into deeper intimacy with You. I want all that You have for me. Please fill me up right now to overflowing with Your Spirit. Please activate my senses and Your supernatural gifts and talents in my life. I welcome You into the deepest parts of my heart, and I give you full permission to take control over my will, emotions, and mind. I ask You to fill me with Your power and the fruit of Your Spirit so that You can flow through my heart and life and be glorified in and through me. In Jesus' name, amen.*[6]

Notice the verbs in this prayer: *fill, activate, control, flow*. These capture the Spirit's dynamic activity. Stirring isn't passive—it's an active partnership.

Scott Crocker, Cru's National Director for Culture & Mission, explains: "Unlike baptism, which is a one-time occurrence (Ephesians 4:5), filling is something that can happen over and over, time and time again . . . It literally means to *keep on being filled*."[7]

Starting the day with the Spirit is powerful, but checking in throughout the day is crucial. Without regular connection, we can drift into self-reliance, depending on our own abilities instead of the Spirit's power. We may start the day with the Spirit, only to find ourselves disconnected by lunchtime. Or worse—days or weeks can pass without us actively pursuing our relationship with God—and when this happens, we're no longer living a Spirit-directed life.

Paul's words resonate in these moments: "For I have the desire to do what is right, but not the ability to carry it out. For I do not do the good I want, but the evil I do not want is what I keep on doing" (Romans 7:18b–19).

Think of your spiritual life like a fitness app. My app sends reminders throughout the day: *Drink water. Move. Log your healthy dinner.* These prompts help me make choices aligned with my health goals.

We need a similar rhythm with the Spirit—a kind of internal "Spirit app" reminding us to stay connected. By doing so, our decisions will align with His guidance, and we'll be empowered to fulfill God's purpose for us: "For we are God's handiwork, created in Christ Jesus to do good works, which God prepared in advance for us to do" (Ephesians 2:10 NIV).

If we listen closely to the Spirit talking to us throughout the day, we can hear His prompts. *Be compassionate. Show kindness. Encourage that person. Offer to pray with them. Don't say that. Say this instead.*

Take a moment to reflect on the incredible gift of the Holy Spirit. God has given you this life-changing presence to guide, empower, and transform you. Are you securing your relationship with the Spirit? Are you holding tight to Him, just as a football player clings to the ball? Without Him, our efforts are wasted—but with Him, we can run the race set before us with power and purpose.

Don't let sin or busyness cause the Spirit's influence to settle in your life like chocolate syrup at the bottom of a glass of milk. Stir Him up daily! Talk with Him, listen to Him, and invite His power into your day. Staying Spirit-filled equips you to live with purpose and experience the rewarding life God has designed for you.

Kilo

(to watch closely, observe, or examine)

1. When have you felt "sacked" in life, and how did you recover?

2. How well do you know the Holy Spirit? Which of the "Top Ten" works of the Spirit do you need most right now? Take time to read some of the verses listed in that section.

3. Are there any past sins you've struggled to believe Jesus has truly forgiven?

4. Have you ever felt unsure if the Holy Spirit is with you? Use the prayers in this chapter to invite Him into your life or to renew your connection with Him.

Extra Resource

To further invite the Holy Spirit into your life, I've created a playlist of songs that help cultivate an atmosphere of openness and receptivity to His presence. Each song has been carefully chosen to encourage you in your spiritual walk and invite the Holy Spirit to move powerfully in your heart. The songs are designed to:

- *Set the tone for prayer and reflection:* Many of the tracks will help you quiet your heart and mind, preparing you for deeper communication with God.

- *Remind you of God's promises:* Through lyrics that speak of His faithfulness, love, and power, the playlist will help you focus on what the Holy Spirit is doing in your life.

- *Stir your faith and expectancy:* Listening to music that celebrates the presence and power of the Holy Spirit can strengthen your faith and fill you with a greater sense of anticipation for what He will do in and through you.

- *Encourage intimacy with God:* As you immerse yourself in these songs, you'll be reminded of God's desire to draw close to you, helping you build a more intimate relationship with Him.

Visit the following website to get the playlist or scan the QR code below.

https://www.fromhimnotthem.com/resources

10

Restoring Your Connection with God

"Humility is not thinking less of yourself, it's thinking of yourself less."
~ C. S. Lewis

When someone hands me a sewing kit, my brain screams, *Don't give this to me! I don't know what to do with it!* In sixth grade, I had to sew a pillow for a class that emphasized life skills. I picked out rainbow-striped fabric at the store, but that was about the only decision I made on my own. My teacher practically did the rest for me. When I say she helped a lot, I mean *a lot*.

The whole project was a struggle. I couldn't even thread the sewing machine properly. My stitches were messy, and the pillow turned out lumpy. My teacher must have realized sewing wasn't my thing because she gave me a passing grade for effort—not skill.

How do you respond when you're bad at something? Maybe you ask for help, but sometimes, it's easier to avoid trying at all. We might think, *I don't want to mess up and have people laugh at me.* Not being good at something is uncomfortable, so we stay in our safe zones.

But here's the thing: Sitting out doesn't make life more enjoyable. Sure, watching others can be a great way to learn something new, but at some point, you have to join in to really experience it.

This also applies to your relationship with God. Sometimes, our pride holds us back from admitting we don't know much about walking with Him. We look around and think, *Everyone else seems to have this Christian thing figured out. If I try, people might see how much I mess up.*

The truth is, none of us have it all together. We all mess up daily. That's why we need Jesus so much. He's the only one who can help us grow and change.

But admitting our sin isn't always easy. Our hearts tend to make excuses, hide the truth, or downplay our mistakes. We like to think of ourselves as "good people," but the Bible paints a different picture—one that reminds us just how much we all miss the mark of perfection. Psalm 14:3 puts it plainly: "There is none who does good, not even one."

Recognizing how much we need God is a big step in walking closely with Him. Being honest about where we fall short opens the door to let the Holy Spirit do His work in us.

One of the scariest moments in daily life is dropping your phone—especially if it's not in a case. Time seems to slow as it slips from your hand, bounces unpredictably on the ground, and you hold your breath hoping the screen isn't shattered. In that moment, you don't care about the photos you were scrolling through or the text you were writing. The only focus is: *Pick it up and check the damage!*

When we realize we're not living a Spirit-directed life, it's a lot like dropping our phone. The first step is to "pick it up" by reconnecting with the Holy Spirit. Thankfully, unlike your phone screen, the Holy Spirit doesn't crack or break. But we can stop hearing His voice or lose the sense of being led by Him.

There's a stretch of back roads near where my husband grew up that's a cell phone "dead zone." Whenever I drive through that area, my connection always gets messed up. I'll hear my friend say, "Hello? Can you hear me?" I still have service, but the signal is weak, and I can't hear the person I'm talking to clearly.

Why does this happen? Something—like a thick forest—is blocking the signal from reaching my phone. Sin works the same way in our relationship with the Holy Spirit. Things like pride, self-reliance, and ungodly choices block us from hearing Him clearly. We don't lose Him completely, but the connection feels distant or distorted. And when that happens, we miss out on the satisfying life Jesus wants for us. The good news? God's always there, waiting for us to pick up and reconnect.

Carrie was raised in a Christian home, attending church every Sunday with her family. It was all she knew, and for a while, it seemed enough. But when she arrived at college, something changed. The love and satisfaction she had felt at home were suddenly missing, and she realized something important: Simply showing up to church wasn't enough.

At first, her choices seemed harmless. She began skipping church on Sundays, and before long, she was caught up in the college party scene. The drinking escalated to dangerous levels—one night, she drank so much she genuinely feared for her life. Even when she regretted her actions the next day, the cycle continued, night after night. With alcohol came other destructive habits, pulling her further from God.

Despite the fun and sense of belonging she found in the social scene, something was missing. The more she chased fulfillment in partying and worldly pleasures, the emptier she felt. The temporary highs faded, leaving behind guilt, pain, and sorrow that only grew with time.

It wasn't until much later that Carrie realized she had been searching for the wrong thing all along. Looking back, she saw that the answer had always been there—found in Christ, not in fleeting pleasures. As she turned back to God, seeking His love and guidance, she finally discovered the deep satisfaction she had been missing. Now, she describes her heart as fully anchored in Christ, living every moment for Him.

❧

Have you ever been part of a group project that spiraled out of control? Maybe someone didn't pull their weight, missed a deadline, or blamed others when things went wrong. It's rare to be part of a team where everyone contributes equally and takes full responsibility. But thinking through what makes group dynamics work—and what makes them fail—can give us a clearer picture of how we should handle our own mistakes, especially when it comes to sin.

Can you imagine a student casually walking away after forgetting to submit their part of the group project, muttering, "No big deal!" That's ridiculous, right? Missing a key piece can derail the entire project and harm everyone's grade. A responsible team member would immediately jump into action, apologizing and working to fix the situation.

In the same way, our sin isn't something to downplay or ignore. It affects more than just us; it strains our relationship with God and can impact others around us. Instead of shrugging it off, we need to recognize its weight and turn to God, not with excuses, but with a heart willing to repent and restore what's been broken.

Now picture a team member standing in front of the group saying, "It's not my fault we're behind schedule—you didn't remind me!" That kind of attitude wouldn't get far with the rest of the group—or the teacher.

When I say things like, "I'm sorry I (fill in the blank), but *you* (fill in the blank)," I'm doing the same thing—blaming others instead of taking responsibility for my actions. A better approach would be to admit, "Sorry, that was my fault. How can I help fix it?"

Likewise, excusing our sin by pointing fingers doesn't make it disappear. Instead of justifying or deflecting, real growth happens when we humbly acknowledge our wrongs and seek to make things right.

Now imagine complaining to the teacher, "The instructions for the project weren't clear, so that's why I didn't do my part." Would the teacher accept that excuse? Probably not! A responsible student would ask questions or seek clarification early on, not use confusion as an excuse for inaction.

But don't we do the same thing in our relationship with God? We defend sinful choices in an attempt to justify our behavior.

"I felt overwhelmed at work and the pressure built up, so I sent a nasty email / yelled at a coworker / gossiped about my boss or colleague."

"That person cut me off in traffic, so I cussed them out / flipped them off / tailgated them to teach them a lesson."

"I couldn't control my sexual feelings, so I looked at (fill in the blank) / I had sex with (fill in the blank) / I cheated on (fill in the blank)."

When we stop making allowances for sin and bring it to Him instead, He meets us with grace, forgiveness, and the power to walk in freedom.

Did you notice the sneaky little word *so* in all those examples? It's a word we often use to rationalize attitudes and actions that don't align with "growing in every way more and more like Christ" (Ephesians 4:15 NLT).

Think about it. When we say something like, "There was no food in the refrigerator at home, so I went to the store and bought groceries," the second part of the sentence makes sense because it logically follows the first.

But sin doesn't follow healthy logic. When we use *so* to justify sin, we're claiming that what we did was reasonable, understandable, and even acceptable. Sin loves to twist logic, making wrong actions seem like the only option.

With most of my life accomplishments, I've felt confident I'd succeed—except for that sixth-grade sewing project! I always believed that if I studied hard enough, I'd get good grades. If I practiced enough, I'd become a great athlete. If I was outgoing, I'd have a lot of friends. That mindset wasn't just my own—it was reinforced by the world around me. Our DIY culture tells us that nothing is out of reach, and growing up, I often heard encouraging slogans like, "You can do anything you set your mind to!" Or, "You have the power within you to achieve anything you want!"[1]

These messages sound nice, but they can be misleading. They put all the focus on *you*—your abilities, your effort, your power. And sometimes, they leave little room for God.

When I applied to intern with a campus ministry at Towson University, one of the staff members who reviewed my application said I was "one of the most capable people she had ever interviewed." At the time, I felt proud—maybe too proud. That comment inflated my ego and made me think I had everything under control.

But years later, after some painful failures and mistakes, I realized some important things about "being capable." Being capable doesn't mean you're honest about your weaknesses. Being capable doesn't mean you're connected to the Holy Spirit. And being capable doesn't mean you're relying on Jesus.

In fact, being capable can make it *harder* to rely on the Spirit.

When you feel capable, it's easier to fake a close relationship with God—even when you're stuck in a destructive cycle of sin, shame, shallow repentance, and more sin. You might keep serving God on the outside, but inside, your heart could be distant or even defiant. People may not notice because appearing capable wins approval. It shields you from hard questions about your moral or spiritual life. But only for so long.

Isabella glared at me across the tiny table at our local coffee shop. If looks could kill, I'd be dead. I'd invited her to talk, even bought her a fancy drink, hoping to create an environment where she felt safe and cared for. She was a gifted student leader—great at facilitating small groups, gathering women for events, and offering thoughtful insights in meetings. But she was also entangled in a pattern of sin with her boyfriend.

This wasn't our first conversation about it. Her choices were compromising both her integrity and her witness. But this time, I knew words alone weren't enough—there had to be a consequence. We asked her to step down from leadership.

She was livid. Arms crossed, jaw clenched, she radiated defensiveness and wounded pride. Her biggest concern wasn't her walk with God or how this might affect her future marriage—whether with her current boyfriend or someone else. She cared most about what others would think when they found out she was no longer a leader.

I can relate to Isabella because I've been in her shoes when overconfidence masked deeper issues. How about you? In what areas of life do you feel capable? Does it help or hinder your walk with God? And when you rely on your own strength, what might you be missing in your relationship with Him?

Then there's been times when I found myself on the other end of the spectrum—feeling anything *but* capable. For instance, when I was writing this book, I struggled with feelings of inadequacy. I often felt emotionally weak, fragile, and unsure of myself. Sometimes, I cried without knowing the reason why. I spent several years pouring time and energy into this project without knowing if it would ever become anything. Would anyone want to read it? Would it all be a waste of time?

In those moments of doubt, I didn't try to impress God with a checklist of accomplishments. Instead, I brought my fears and weaknesses to Him. I prayed, "God, I need You. I can't do this without You."

And that's exactly where God wants us to be: honest, dependent, and humble. As John reminds us: "If we say we have no sin, we deceive ourselves, and the truth is not in us. *If we confess our sins*, he is faithful and just to forgive us our sins and to cleanse us from all unrighteousness" (1 John 1:8–9, emphasis mine).

Moving from focusing on being capable to confessional helps us rely on God and stay connected to Him.

❦

When we mess up, the best way to respond is with humility. When we sin, pride often rushes in, making it harder to have a soft heart that's receptive to correction. We think we're protecting ourselves, but pride actually sabotages our connection with God, leaving us weaker, not stronger.

James points out this truth in his letter: "God opposes the proud but gives grace to the humble" (4:6). Pride creates distance from God, while humility invites His grace and favor. A humble heart is essential for living in harmony with God and recovering from our failures.

You've probably heard the phrase "eat humble pie." It's often used to describe someone who's been brought low through their own pride—like an overconfident athlete losing in a humiliating defeat. But wouldn't it be better to start with humility? When we adopt a humble disposition, we can more easily acknowledge mistakes and move forward without the extra baggage of pride.

When we think about God, His power is often the first thing that comes to mind. But consider this: Jesus described Himself as "gentle and lowly in heart" (Matthew 11:29). If anyone had the right to claim exaltation, it was Jesus, the Son of God. Yet, He chose humility as the foundation of His life and ministry.

This is the side of Jesus we need to remember when dealing with our failures. When we stumble, humility is what allows us to confess, reconnect with God, and move forward. Jesus' own example reminds us that humility isn't weakness—it's the path to grace, strength, and restoration.

Kyle "Quilly" Quilausing went from Hawaii's six-time state golf champion to a name on the Hawaii's Most Wanted list. He's someone who let pride and bad choices ruin his dreams. After an altercation with a teacher got him kicked out of high school, Kyle became addicted to crystal meth in his twenties, went to jail, escaped, and ended up serving a ten-year prison sentence—with three of those years spent in solitary confinement.[2]

While in prison, Kyle's life changed. He now calls himself "a servant of God," "a family man," and "a man of integrity." His motto, "Stay Humble Pray," became his lifeline, especially during his time in solitary confinement when he thought he might go crazy.

Now, Kyle is a motivational speaker who warns young people about the dangers of drugs. His message has reached hundreds of thousands of students across Hawaii, who proudly display his motto "Stay Humble Pray" on T-shirts, hoodies, and bumper stickers.

My husband met Kyle to talk to him about speaking at the University of Hawaii-Hilo, where we worked with college students. Kyle shared a gripping story about reaching his lowest point in jail, when he heard voices telling him to harm himself. In that dark moment, his encounter with Jesus and the simple refrain "Stay Humble Pray" gave him hope and strength.

Kyle's story reminds us that humility and prayer are not just slogans—they're lifelines. Staying humble and praying helped Kyle rebuild his life and stay connected to God. "Stay Humble Pray" can be our lifeline too.

Sipping an Americano, I sighed deeply, letting the beauty of the bay calm the storm in my soul. That morning, I'd tried to share with Tim my desire for a closer relationship. We weren't doing date nights anymore, and we weren't really spending time with each other. Our efforts seemed focused on driving the kids to their sporting events and meeting their needs. I wanted quality time with my husband. But when I tried to express this, my words came out all wrong. Instead of drawing us closer, my frustration spilled out as a hurtful verbal attack. I felt the distance between us expand, and regret settled in my chest.

Then the sharp, jarring sound of a weed whacker broke through the peaceful morning. The soft coos of birds, the laughter of families, and the lapping of waves were drowned out. If you've ever been woken up on a Saturday morning by your neighbor's lawn mower, you know exactly what it felt like.

I wanted to cover my ears and shout, "Make it stop!" But I couldn't. Short of asking the park worker to abandon his duties, there were only two choices: Endure the noise or leave. I left.

As I walked away, I realized something: My sin is like that weed whacker. It fractures peace, disrupts harmony, and breaks relationships—both with God and with others.

Who in your life feels distant because of unresolved conflict? What's standing in the way of peace between you and that person? Are you willing to tolerate sin, or are you ready to take action to address it? What steps can you take today to begin healing and restoring peace in your relationships?

Restoring closeness and trust in a relationship isn't always easy, but it's worth the effort. Later that day, I made the choice to talk with Tim about our earlier argument. Let's just say it required a little humility—admitting I'd been too harsh wasn't fun, but I knew I needed to own my words and how they hurt him.

Once we addressed the tension between us, we could revisit the real issue: how to prioritize our relationship despite the chaos of parenting. The truth was, I had expected Tim to read my mind—to just *know* what I wanted without me having to say it. When that didn't happen, I let frustration build instead of simply communicating my needs. That conversation, as uncomfortable as it was at first, ended up strengthening our connection rather than fracturing it further.

Early in my marriage, someone shared with me a way of thinking about intimacy that has stuck with me. Think of it this way: *In-To-Me-See*. Intimacy means allowing someone to see the deepest, most vulnerable parts of you—your hopes and fears, dreams and doubts, joys and anxieties. It's an incredible privilege to be fully known and loved.

Timothy Keller explains it this way in his book about marriage: "To be loved but not known is comforting but superficial. To be known and not loved is our greatest fear. But to be fully known and truly loved is, well, a lot like being loved by God. It is what we need more than anything."[3]

God knows you fully. He sees into the very depths of your heart. And He loves you. The prophet Zephaniah assures, "The Lord your God is with you, the Mighty Warrior who saves. He will take great delight in you; in his love he will no longer rebuke you, but will rejoice over you with singing (Zephaniah 3:17 NIV).

God isn't interested in a checklist of do's and don'ts. He's seeking intimacy with you—a relationship built on honesty, trust, and connection.

When sin ruptures your relationship with God, don't let shame or pride keep you from addressing it. Think about the steps you need to take to restore harmony:

- **Acknowledge the noise.** Recognize how sin disrupts your connection with God and others.

- **Confess and repair.** Admit where you've gone wrong, and take steps to make it right.

- **Draw near.** Seek God's forgiveness and allow Him to restore your relationship.

It's in that closeness with God—when you're fully known and fully loved—that you'll find peace again.

If you'll bear with me, I have one more football analogy (plus I know some of you women enjoy football just as much as men!). We can draw inspiration from one of the greatest NFL quarterbacks of all time: Brett Favre. Known for his incredible passing skills, Favre holds the unique record of throwing for over 70,000 yards, 500 touchdowns, 300 interceptions, 6,000 completions, and 10,000 pass attempts—a feat unmatched in NFL history.[4]

But here's the twist: Brett Favre also holds the record for the most fumbles. His fumbles didn't disqualify him from setting records. He didn't give up after a mistake or let his errors define him. Instead, he kept showing up, kept throwing, and built a career so remarkable that he earned his spot in the Pro Football Hall of Fame.

The Bible has its own "Hall of Faith," recorded in Hebrews 11. This chapter highlights men and women who weren't perfect but persevered in faith. Their lives were marked not by their failures but by their unwavering resolve to follow God despite their mistakes.

RESTORING YOUR CONNECTION WITH GOD   173

Consider some of the individuals included:

- **Moses** killed an Egyptian in anger yet led Israel out of slavery.

- **David**, a man after God's own heart, committed adultery and murder, yet repented and continued to seek God.

- **Rahab**, a prostitute, acted in faith and helped secure victory for God's people.

Their stories remind us that no failure is final when paired with repentance and a determination to walk with God.

Like the heroes of faith, we will stumble. But the story doesn't end there. Proverbs 24:16 offers this encouragement: "For the righteous falls seven times and rises again..."

This verse doesn't promise perfection. Instead, it promises *perseverance*. A righteous person isn't defined by the number of times they fall but by their commitment to rise again, to restore their connection with God, and to walk by the Spirit.

When we recognize our mistakes and our distance from God, we can take immediate steps to reconnect with Him. Here are two prayers to help realign your heart with His Spirit:

> *God, my sin matters! I confess that at times I act like a person who doesn't know You. I admit I (fill in the blank). Please forgive me and help me to depend on You fully. Thank You for loving me and giving me another chance to follow You.*

> *Jesus, I admit I haven't been in step with You. In seeking to control my life, I have (insert specific sin). This was wrong, and I'm sorry for grieving You. Thank You for forgiving me. Please direct and empower me. Help me to want what You want for my life and give me the courage and strength to live obediently.*

These moments of prayer help us rise again, just like the righteous described in Proverbs.

Mistakes happen. It's part of being human, but they don't have to define your future. Whether you're in a season of weakness, caught in a cycle of sin, or feeling distant from God, remember that restoration is possible. Like Kyle Quilausing, Brett Favre, the heroes of faith, and countless others who stumbled but kept going, you have the power to persevere. No matter where you are in your journey, God's grace and the Holy Spirit's strength are always available to help you rise again. Take a moment today to invite God to restore your connection with Him. Let His grace renew your heart, and trust that He will guide you forward, no matter the obstacles you face. You don't have to do it alone—He's with you, ready to help you move forward in faith.

And as you restore your connection with God, know that there's even more He wants for you. In the final chapter, we'll dive into how you can strengthen yourself spiritually and build the habits that will allow you to stay firmly grounded in Him—no matter the circumstances. It's time to take your spiritual life to the next level, and you won't want to miss what's ahead.

Kilo

(to watch closely, observe, or examine)

1. What kind of image do you think others expect from Christians?

2. Where have you minimized, blamed, or excused sin recently? Is there a *so* involved?

3. In what areas of life do you feel capable? Does this help or hinder your walk with God?

4. Who are you struggling to stay close to? What can you do to repair that relationship?

5. Read Hebrews 11. Who stands out, and what are they remembered for?

Extra Resource

If you've found this chapter helpful, I encourage you to download my devotion on the importance of practicing faith falls. Download it today and start practicing the spiritual strength that comes from falling with faith.

Visit the following website to read my "Practicing Faith Falls" devotion or scan the QR code below.

https://www.fromhimnotthem.com/resources

11

Overcoming the Opposition
with the Holy Spirit

**"You, LORD, are mighty, and your faithfulness
surrounds You. You rule over the surging sea;
when its waves mount up, You still them."
~ Psalm 89:8b-9 NIV**

Working on her surfing skills at one of our outdoor student ministry events, Ava struggled to get back to shore. Pummeling waves had separated her from her friends, and a strong current made it hard to swim directly to shore—especially as fatigue washed over her. As Ava relayed the story to us, she trembled as she relived her panic and fear.

Then her face shone as she said, "At my weakest point, He was there!" At just the moment she thought she was going under, she cried out to God for help. Immediately, she made eye contact with a man who materialized out of nowhere. Barely, she managed a small, frantic wave. The swimmer quickly cut through the waves and grabbed her, towing her into safety.

Here's the thing: When Ava had calmed down enough on the beach to thank her rescuer, he had disappeared. He wasn't back in the water, nor anywhere along the shore. Despite this being a scary event, Ava believes God rescued her (possibly even using an angel), which bolstered her growing newfound faith.

As someone who had been exposed to very little Scripture growing up, Ava was not familiar with the Bible story in Matthew

14 of the disciples who ran into trouble when their boat was tossed about by a storm. Together, we read the story of how Jesus appeared to them walking on the waves and how Peter stepped out in faith on the surface to walk toward Jesus.

Ava was struck by the similarity of her story with Peter's: They both sank when they focused on the waves. Yet Matthew records that as the waters closed over Peter's head, Jesus immediately stretched out His hand and lifted him up (14:31). The moment both Peter and Ava switched their gaze to Jesus and cried out for help, He was there!

We praised God together that Jesus is always watching and eager to help. He says the same thing to you that He said to Peter. "Be brave and don't be afraid. I am here!" (v. 27 TPT). Jesus knows where you are and what you're dealing with, even if all you can see is a storm.

We know life is full of storms, both physical and spiritual. Just as we need to prepare for real storms, we must also stay ready for the challenges we face in our faith. But *how* we prepare matters. We don't strengthen ourselves by relying on our own wisdom, willpower, or emotions. We don't find stability by following anxiety, forcing our way through, or turning to counterfeit spiritual guides. Instead, we must anchor ourselves in Christ and allow the Holy Spirit to lead us. In this final chapter, we'll explore what it means to stand firm—not in our own strength, but in His—and how staying spiritually strong begins with surrendering to the guidance of the Spirit, who empowers us to overcome the enemy's attacks and resist the opposition that seeks to shake our faith.

I once heard a radio show where people shared tips for surviving tornadoes. One caller from Oklahoma, a place nicknamed

"Tornado Alley," gave this advice: Make sure your phone is fully charged before the storm hits. Why? Because if you lose power, you'll be disconnected from the outside world. If there's an emergency, you'll need a way to call for help.

That advice stuck with me. It's a great picture of how we need to stay spiritually "charged"—connected to God and filled with His power through the Holy Spirit. Without Him, we are weak and exposed. When we're empowered by the Spirit, we're better protected. But if we lose that connection, we're left wide open to attacks—not just from outside forces but also from ourselves.

Have you ever made a bad choice and thought later, *Why did I do that?* Maybe you:

- Put off a big assignment and got a bad grade.

- Overscheduled yourself and missed something important.

- Spent too much money and couldn't pay a bill.

- Said something rude and got a harsh response.

- Stayed up too late and were exhausted the next day.

Sometimes, our worst enemy isn't someone else—it's us. The Bible calls this our "flesh," or our human tendency to sin. When we try to live life without the Spirit's help, we often make a mess of things.

Andrea had one guiding motto for her life: *I do me.* Growing up without close connections to her parents (she couldn't remember ever having met her dad, and she wasn't close to her mom), Andrea had learned to trust in herself. This meant she lived her authentic self, making choices based upon what *she* thought or felt was good for her. She believed if she looked inward to her true self that she could create the positive life she desired.

Yet she burned through relationships, looking for love. In high school, she never went more than six months without dating. Then she ended up alone and pregnant, wondering how operating in her own strength and wisdom could have gone so badly. It took well over a year for Andrea to accept that she could not save herself and was in need of a savior. After trusting in Christ for eternal life, Andrea had to learn a new way of living, of recognizing the Holy Spirit talking to her, guiding her, and empowering her.

The Bible says, "If we live by the Spirit, let us also keep in step with the Spirit" (Galatians 5:25). Jesus is our perfect example. The Holy Spirit filled Him and gave Him power (Luke 3:21–22, 4:1). He didn't face temptation or begin His ministry without the Spirit. He showed us how to live every day in complete dependence on God.

Think about the things you never leave home without. Maybe it's your phone, makeup, or a water bottle. If you live in a colder climate, it's warm gloves and a beanie. My phone's battery dies pretty quickly, so I carry a power bank with me. We prioritize these items because we don't want to be caught unprepared. The same is true spiritually.

What if we made a choice to never leave home without the Holy Spirit?

The Spirit isn't just an optional "nice-to-have." He's essential. We can't navigate life's challenges, grow in our faith, or live out God's purposes without Him. So, stay connected. Stay "charged." And don't leave home without Him! Remember, you can follow the prayer prompts at the end of Chapter 9 to activate His power and presence on an ongoing basis in your life.

❦

Have you ever played a sport where someone played dirty? Maybe it was that kid on the opposing team who tripped you when the ref wasn't looking or the one who twisted the rules just enough to get away with it. We all know someone like that! Someone who bends or breaks the rules to get ahead, no matter how unfair it is. They'll do whatever it takes to secure a win, even if it means hurting others or destroying the integrity of the game. It's frustrating, isn't it? It makes you feel like no matter how hard you play, the odds are stacked against you.

We have a spiritual enemy who doesn't play by the rules either. And his goal is to take us out—not just from the game of life but from the mission God has given us.

In the book of Revelation, John is shown a heavenly battle where Satan, "the great dragon," is cast down to earth (Revelation 12:9). The Bible also calls him "the deceiver of the whole world" and "the accuser of our brothers" (vv. 9–10). Now, knowing his time is short, he wages war on those "who keep the commandments of God and hold to the testimony of Jesus" (v. 17).

During the pandemic, do you remember being reminded of the importance of using hand sanitizer? Many stores wouldn't let you enter until you'd sanitized your hands. It was all about keeping things clean and safe. But here's the reality: Satan cannot be sanitized. No amount of spin, modernity, or intellectualism can clean up his image. Scripture makes his nature unmistakably clear. Consider some of his attributes:

- **Lies** (John 8:44)

- **Deceives** (Genesis 3:4–5)

- **Condemns** (1 Timothy 3:6)

- **Blinds people from knowing the truth** (2 Corinthians 4:4)

- **Waits for the right moment to attack** (Luke 4:13)

- **Accuses brothers and sisters in Christ** (Revelation 12:10)

- **Is a thief who comes only to steal, kill, and destroy** (John 10:10a)

We're vulnerable to spiritual attack, but one of the main ways the Holy Spirit guides us is by giving us the strength to fight back. Without Him, we're like unarmed soldiers in the middle of a war.

Even Jesus faced attacks from Satan. After resisting the devil's temptations in the wilderness, the Bible says, "He departed from Jesus until an opportune time" (Luke 4:13). Satan was waiting for another moment when Jesus might be weak. But, "Jesus returned *in the power of the Spirit* ... and a report about him went out through all the surrounding country" (v. 14, emphasis mine).

Think about how hard it must have been for Jesus as He approached the cross. He faced betrayal by His friends, denial by Peter, and the abandonment of His closest followers. Yet, Jesus stayed firm. He didn't give in to the enemy's attacks, and He didn't deviate from His mission. Jesus didn't face the cross alone. He continued to be led and strengthened by the Holy Spirit.

You know what? Satan still works the same way today. He waits for moments when we are weak, distracted, or disconnected from God. It's easy for a relationship with God to slip down the priority list. Melissa was consumed with soccer, hoping for a college scholarship. Jordan focused on maintaining her GPA to keep her academic scholarship. Tamara loved volunteering and attended school club events almost every night. While none of these pursuits are bad, they can overshadow our connection with God.

And that's exactly when Satan strikes—when we're too busy, too tired, or too focused on everything but God. He doesn't need us to reject our faith outright; he just wants to keep us spiritually weak and off course. When we're not communicating with God, we're more likely to believe one of Satan's lies.

But we don't have to be defenseless. The Spirit gives us the strength to resist temptation, the courage to stand firm, and the wisdom to navigate life's challenges. Without Him, we are unprotected and easily swayed. With Him, we are grounded, empowered, and ready to recognize the enemy's tactics before they take hold.

Staying filled with the Spirit and allowing Him to lead us requires consistent attention—much like maintaining a vehicle, as I realized during an unforgettable moment with my van.

"I think the van is on fire!" I told my husband alarmingly over the phone.

"What do you see? Are there flames? Do you see smoke?" Tim probed.

Clouds of dark smoke billowed from both sides of the van's rear through the wheel wells. The acrid smell assaulted my nostrils. After I relayed the information to Tim, he asked, "Is the parking brake on?" in a carefully controlled voice.

Sigh. I hadn't checked that. A quick peek at the parking brake confirmed Tim's suspicion: I had just driven with it on for the last twenty minutes!

This is not the first time I've called Tim about car-related issues. It's a demonstration of his patience and self-control that he didn't initially reply, "What do you MEAN the van is on fire?" Instinctively, I already knew I had caused the problem.

Tim has had many conversations with me over the years about my need for vehicle awareness. It might be a missed flashing light on the dashboard, my tendency to narrowly make it to the gas station before I'm on empty, or my failure to report an unusual noise. *What noise? There was a noise?*

I wonder if Tim identifies with how the author of Hebrews must have felt when he addressed first-century Jewish Christians and their spiritual immaturity:

I have a lot more to say about this, but it is hard to get it across to you since you've picked up this bad habit of not listening. By this time you ought to be teachers yourselves, yet here I find you need someone to sit down with you and go over the basics on God again, starting from square one—baby's milk, when you should have been on solid food long ago! Milk is for beginners, inexperienced in God's ways; solid food is for the mature, who have some practice in telling right from wrong. (5:11–14 msg)

Swallowing my pride, I asked Tim to review the basics with me. What I discovered went way beyond information (helpful as it was). He has a different mindset than me, and dare I say, *relationship* with our vehicles.

I don't start paying attention until something is wrong.

This approach is extremely costly. The resulting problem may be financial: We may need an expensive new transmission, or, heaven forbid, I destroy the car to the extent that it's not fixable and we need to buy a new car. Or the problem may be bodily: Due to my laziness, an accident occurs, and someone is physically hurt. Our lives could be at stake.

Conversely, Tim pays attention to our vehicles so that things go right.

Almost every day, he walks out to our cars and inspects them. He examines the tires. Sometimes, he checks the oil. He thinks about things like fluid changes and part replacements. Astonishingly, he keeps a running mental list of next tasks.

In comparison, I mentally carry only the bare information I need to maintain my desired relationship with our vehicles. Sheepishly, I've realized I have more of a parasitic connection with them than I care to admit. They serve me. Only when they no longer function for me the way I expect and want them to do I sit up and take notice.

Additionally, my disengagement is only made possible because *someone else* takes care of our vehicles and properly maintains them. I take advantage of the fact that Tim pays attention to the cars, so I don't have to.

Might those be the same reasons the writer of Hebrews chastised his readers?

Perhaps their bad habit of not listening stemmed from how they interacted similarly with God.

We pay attention and listen *when we care.*

We act *when we believe we are personally responsible.*

Therefore, we must ask ourselves some hard questions.

Do we care about our relationship with God? Do we value our connection enough to dedicate the time, attention, and energy to relate to Him healthily? Do we believe something valuable is at stake if we don't?

Have we relied upon someone else to spoon-feed us instead of owning our spiritual growth and maturity? Do we read the Word ourselves? Or is it good enough that someone (typically a pastor) puts in the hard work of studying and feeds it to us once a week?

You may be feeling uncomfortable right now, like I did after being confronted with these realities. However, if we want to strengthen ourselves spiritually, we must prioritize our relationship with God.

Here are seven practical steps you can take to move from being spiritually immature to having a vibrant, growing relationship with God—one where you actively listen to His voice, follow His leading, and rely on the Holy Spirit for wisdom, strength, and direction.

1. **Evaluate your spiritual attention.** Reflect on whether you're actively engaged in your relationship with God or passively relying on others to maintain it for you.

2. **Embrace healthy conviction.** If you recognize areas of neglect in your spiritual life, don't ignore those feelings.

Use them as motivation to make changes.

3. **Develop a desire for ownership.** Cultivate a longing to know God personally and take responsibility for growing in your faith.

4. **Create a "daily inspection" routine.** This could include reading Scripture, praying intentionally, and/or journaling about what God is teaching you.

5. **Own your spiritual growth.** Commit to studying God's Word for yourself rather than only relying on others. You could choose a Bible reading plan or devotional to follow consistently. One great option is to listen to the free audio Bible in relatable women's voices, using the *her.BIBLE* app.[1] Or join a Bible study group where you actively participate and engage.

6. **Set spiritual maintenance goals.** Identify specific steps you can take to mature in your faith, such as memorizing key Bible verses, prioritizing worship and serving others regularly, or being accountable to a mentor or friend who encourages your growth.

7. **Take responsibility for your influence.** Recognize that your growth impacts others. Whether it's your family, friends, or peers, decide to lead by example in showing what it looks like to pursue God wholeheartedly.

Spiritual neglect leaves us vulnerable—drifting through life without the strength, wisdom, and guidance we need. But when we stay connected to the Holy Spirit, we are empowered to stand firm, resist temptation, and navigate life's challenges with confidence. Just as maintaining a vehicle requires ongoing care and attention, so does maintaining our relationship with God. By taking intentional steps to grow in faith, we move from passivity to purpose, from dependence on others to a thriving, personal connection with God. As you commit to this journey, remember: The Holy Spirit is always present, ready to guide, strengthen, and sustain you every step of the way.

While attending a ministry conference at Colorado State University in Fort Collins, Colorado, my family decided to take a break for a scenic drive and hike. My daughters soon began asking for snacks, so I handed Taylor a mini cashew cookie-flavor Larabar. I didn't think much of it—until Taylor took a bite and her body immediately reacted.

Taylor had experienced severe allergies as a baby. Her reactions ranged from eczema and hives to asthma attacks that once sent us rushing to the hospital. After one particularly scary episode, the doctors nearly intubated her and suggested an airlift to Johns Hopkins Hospital. Thankfully, she recovered, but we learned through testing that Taylor was allergic to eggs, dairy, gluten, nuts, cats, and dogs.

As Taylor grew, some of her allergies improved, and the big reactions seemed to fade. Over time, I got lax about checking food labels, assuming we'd outgrown the worst. I knew on paper she was allergic to cashews, but she had never actually eaten one—until now.

As Taylor's symptoms worsened, my husband turned the rental van around, racing down the mountain as fast as possible. Taylor's discomfort grew, and we didn't have her EpiPen or even any Benadryl with us. To make matters worse, our phones had no service. All we could do was pray and keep moving, unsure if her reaction would escalate to anaphylaxis.

"I'm going to throw up!" Taylor cried from the backseat. My husband stopped, and Taylor threw open the door, purging everything she had eaten. Miraculously, that stopped the reaction from progressing further. Though her throat stayed clear, we still headed into town in case she needed medical attention.

Looking back, I realized how unprepared we were. The entire episode could have ended much differently. But after this close call, I became more vigilant—for a time. Yet, as the years passed, I grew careless again. Twice since then, I've mistakenly given Taylor food containing cashews. Each time, I've asked myself, *Why didn't I stay on high alert?*

Because the threat felt distant, I let my guard down.

⚜

We often make similar mistakes in our spiritual battle with evil. Like the military leaders at Pearl Harbor who deemed an attack by Japan unlikely, we underestimate our enemy. We misjudge Satan's resourcefulness and determination, assuming he won't attack or we're too strong to fall—until the headlines remind us otherwise, telling of yet another respected spiritual leader caught in sin. Beyond these shocking announcements, others in our churches and ministries also give in to temptation. It's common to hear about someone committing adultery, stealing from their organization, or abusing power for personal gain.

We shouldn't be surprised at these spiritual failures because the Bible warns us we are living in a real spiritual battle. Paul reminds us in Ephesians 6:12, "For we do not wrestle against flesh and blood, but against the rulers, against the authorities, against the cosmic powers over this present darkness, against the spiritual forces of evil in the heavenly places." Our battle is not against visible enemies but against a cunning, unseen adversary.

Just as I became careless with Taylor's allergies, we can grow complacent in our spiritual vigilance. The devil is always looking for an opportune moment to strike, whether through subtle temptations, distractions, or outright attacks. When we let down our guard, we leave ourselves exposed.

Thankfully, Scripture provides us with "intelligence" about the enemy's strategies. It also equips us with everything we need to stand firm in God's truth. Ephesians 6:13–20 describes the "armor of God" given to us for protection: truth, righteousness, faith, salvation, and the Word of God. These aren't just concepts—*they are practical tools for everyday battles.*

❧

The flu bug hit us hard. Our oldest daughter, just shy of her second birthday, came down with it first. My husband and I caught it shortly after, and to complicate matters, I was in my ninth month of pregnancy with our second child. To top it off, a winter storm dumped thirteen inches of snow, creating four-foot-high icy walls behind our cars.

What if I went into labor? My husband was too sick to shovel, and I certainly couldn't do it in my condition.

Cue the heroic arrival of my brother and sister-in-law! After plowing their farm lane (no small task), they cautiously drove twenty minutes through dangerous conditions to reach us. Once at our home, they shoveled our entire driveway in the freezing cold, wind whipping snow in every direction. They even left a pot of homemade chicken noodle soup, Gatorade, and disinfectant wipes just inside the front door.

They were true servants. Yet here's the humbling part—*I didn't even remember it.* It wasn't until *years* later, as I reread an old journal entry, that the memory came back to me.

Why did I forget?

I'd like to blame it on pregnancy brain, but I think it speaks to a deeper truth about human nature: *We are prone to forgetfulness.* Even extraordinary acts of kindness can fade from our memories.

This is often when Satan assaults us. When we don't remember God's kindness and faithfulness, He whispers lies that we start to believe. *God doesn't love you. He's forgotten about you. It's pointless to ask Him for help.*

The Bible, though, calls us to a different way of living: *remembering*. Faith is unleashed when we remember, because remembering strengthens our connection to God, fuels our faith—which pleases Him—and gives us the courage to trust Him in our current trials. While I've discussed elsewhere in this book the importance of knowing, memorizing, and declaring Scripture, as well as praying to strengthen yourself spiritually, remembering stands as a powerful spiritual weapon in its own right.

When God rescued the Israelites from slavery in Egypt, Moses urged them to "remember this day in which you came out from Egypt, out of the house of slavery, for by a strong hand the Lord brought you out from this place" (Exodus 13:3). Remembering God's faithfulness fosters worship, softens our hearts toward Him, and motivates us to serve and obey Him.

In a world where we tend to fixate on the future, we can benefit from looking back. It's a spiritual practice that requires intentionality and focus. Remembering how God has been faithful in the past strengthens our trust in Him for the present and the future. As we recall His guidance, provision, and truth, our faith is reinforced, making us more attuned to the Holy Spirit's leading and less susceptible to the deception of counterfeit guides.

Here are a few good ways we can remember:

- **Recollect:** Spend time in prayer, asking God to bring to mind specific moments from the past year(s) when you experienced His goodness. Ask yourself, *How did God move in unexpected ways? Where have I seen His hand of provision, protection, or guidance? How has He answered my prayers or shown His faithfulness?*

- **Record:** Write these moments down in a journal or create a visual reminder, like a gratitude jar or a list on your fridge, to revisit throughout the year. Annually, on Thanksgiving Day, my family records the big things we're thankful for from the past year in a special book. Each year, we look back on notes from five, ten, fifteen years ago and remember how God moved in our lives. I also record my gratitude throughout the year for smaller—but no less significant—ways God has shown up in a separate journal.

- **Recount:** Share these memories with others. Post about them on your socials. Grab coffee with a friend. Instead of moaning about everything going wrong in your life, praise God for how He's been at work. Talking about God's faithfulness encourages not only your heart but also the hearts of those around you.

As we come to the final part of this journey, I want to remind you of what we've explored together: the importance of turning to God—not others—for your validation, identity, and guidance. Throughout this book, we've talked about how God's mission for us can only be fully embraced when we walk in the power of the Holy Spirit. It's through Him that we are equipped to live out the calling He has placed on our lives.

It's crucial to remember that staying connected to the Spirit isn't just for our personal strength or peace. The gift of the Holy Spirit was never intended to be an end in itself; it's always been paired with a mission. As Luke records, Jesus told His disciples: "But you will receive power when the Holy Spirit has come upon you, and *you will be my witnesses* in Jerusalem and in all Judea and Samaria, and to the end of the earth" (Acts 1:8, emphasis mine).

Similarly, John describes the resurrected Jesus commissioning His disciples: "Peace be with you. As the Father has sent me, even so I am sending you." And when he had said this, he breathed on them and said, "Receive the Holy Spirit" (John 20:21–22).

As Heather and Ashley Holleman explain, "*Sent* begins from a starting point of our identity in Christ; evangelism flows from who we are rather than inviting us into something more to do. As a result, we live as sent people not out of guilt, shame, or a sense of duty. Sent people naturally enter into evangelism the same way they eat breakfast or walk down the street."[2]

The devil's ultimate goal is to stop us from being *sent ones.* Why? Because Christians who embrace their identity in Christ and live out their mission with authenticity wield tremendous power. Imagine the transformative impact we could have if introducing others to Jesus became as natural as eating breakfast or walking down the street. Yet, much like Prince Hans in *Frozen* tried to keep Anna from stepping into her true purpose and ruling the kingdom, the enemy works to thwart our God-given calling. He knows that when we embrace our mission, we become unstoppable.

Instead of stepping out in faith, though, we attempt peace negotiations with the devil. We offer compromises—spiritual "desk jobs" of minimal risk and involvement—in exchange for an illusion of safety. We avoid acting in faith, afraid of the cost, and in doing so, we become fruitless servants of the Lord. We may feel "safe," but we're forfeiting the life of purpose and joy that Jesus has for us.

How can we recognize if we've accepted a spiritual desk job?

- We leave sharing our faith to "professionals."

- We produce little or no spiritual fruit.

- We allow fear to define our actions more than faith.

- We neglect prayer and worship.

- We don't know, memorize, or declare God's Word over our lives.

- We avoid anything that requires deep reliance on God.

Ultimately, we fit Paul's description of people in the last days who have "the appearance of godliness, but denying its power" (2 Timothy 3:5).

Yet, time and again in campus ministry, I've witnessed something different—countless Spirit-filled students stepping out of their comfort zones to make a real impact. For example, students who joined the "Tuesday Night Thing" found creative ways to show God's love on campus, like grilling free s'mores or picking up trash. Others spent their summers on worldwide missions, ranging from two to ten weeks, growing in their faith and doing meaningful work like caring for orphans, sharing the gospel with university students, meeting needs of the impoverished in cities, or installing water filters in areas without safe drinking water.

You can be like Beth, who, despite being terrified, trusted God to help her share her faith at a spring break conference with students partying on the beach. Or like Phoebe, who started a small-group Bible study for her sorority. Or Megan, who launched a campus movement at her community college. Or Kate, who found the courage to tell her family she had become a Christian while at college.

This is what happens when we take faith action steps—when we embrace the mission God has for us, like Beth, Phoebe, Megan, and Kate. People notice something different about us. Just like Stacy's friend, who said, "That is what is different about you. I figured it out. You know Jesus!" When we live authentically for Christ, it's clear to others that something has transformed us. And that transformation can inspire them to seek the same life-changing relationship with Him.

Instead of being ineffective, silent witnesses, we can become Spirit-empowered warriors.

For many years, thousands of students at Cru Winter Conferences across the country have signed the following pledge, created by the Campus Ministry:

> *Lord Jesus, I submit to you, and in the power of your Spirit, I will ...*
> *Go where You want me to go.*
> *Do what You want me to do.*
> *Say what You want me to say.*
> *Give where You want me to give.*

In signing the pledge, some accepted Christ into their lives for the first time, others committed to a summer mission trip, and some planned to spend a year in full-time ministry. If you're exploring what it means to be led by the Holy Spirit, start by considering how you can show His love to the people around you—your family, classmates, and teammates. I'm so excited for you! And I can't wait to hear stories of transformation as you step forward in faith, leaning on Him for guidance and walking in the confidence of His love.

I pray that through these pages, you've been reminded that your worth isn't found in the shifting opinions of others but in the unchanging love of the One who created you. You are loved by the Father, led by Jesus, and empowered by the Holy Spirit—an unstoppable force in this spiritual war. The God who sees you is always present, guiding and equipping you to overcome.

Remember, the Spirit empowers us to abandon counterfeit forms of guidance. Feelings don't need to lead the way, nor do we have to take charge of our lives in ways that relegate God to the back seat. Anxiety may demand our attention, but it leads us in circles, not forward. And dabbling in what's spiritually forbidden only pulls us further from the One who offers true guidance and peace. In partnership with the Holy Spirit, we can successfully navigate life—even with limited sight.

As you step forward, may you walk in His strength, live out your purpose, and share His love with a world that so desperately needs it. You are called, chosen, and equipped for this very moment in history. May the peace of Christ rule in your heart, and may His joy be your strength. Go with confidence, knowing that the God Who Sees is always with you—leading, sustaining, and reminding you that everything you need comes *from Him, not them.*

Kilo

(to watch closely, observe, or examine)

1. What's one thing you never leave home without?

2. How can we stay connected to, empowered by, and led by the Holy Spirit?

3. Share a time when you let your guard down. What happened?

4. Read Ephesians 6:13–20. How does missing one piece of armor make us vulnerable?

Extra Resource

As we navigate an ever-changing world, we face unique challenges and pressures. But as Christians, we are not without strength, purpose, or guidance. It's time we stop settling for a life that's just "okay" or "good enough," and instead step into the abundant life that Christ promised. Let's make a conscious decision to embrace the mission God has for us and empower one another in this walk. When we choose to live this way, we impact not only our lives but also the world around us.

You can sign the same surrender pledge referenced in this chapter! Let it be your declaration of your commitment to live intentionally, to follow the Holy Spirit, and to be authentic in your faith journey.

Visit the following website to download a copy of the pledge or scan the QR code below.

https://www.fromhimnotthem.com/resources

Acknowledgments

First, I want to thank **my amazing husband, Tim, and our three daughters.** Your love, patience, and encouragement have been my greatest support. Tim, your eye for detail and willingness to give thoughtful feedback—especially during those tough early drafts—has made all the difference. Thank you for helping with countless duties, from running our daughters to activities to giving me the time and space I needed to write. I'm forever grateful for your unwavering belief in me.

To **my parents and twin sister,** thank you for your love and support. Your persistent encouragement to get this book written, as well as your help in ensuring the accuracy and integrity of the events shared here, means more to me than I can say. Mom and Dad, your legacy of faith and love continues to shape who I am, and I am forever grateful.

To **our faithful ministry partners,** whose prayers and financial support have made it possible for us to serve for over twenty years in full-time ministry—thank you for your generosity and faithfulness. Your partnership not only sustained our ministry but also allowed us to invest in the lives of so many. We couldn't have done this without you.

To **the Cru staff who mentored me and served alongside me in many capacities**—I couldn't possibly thank you all here, but know that your influence and support have shaped my ministry in ways that words can't express.

To **Jim Kercheval and Jen Hu,** whose coaching from the

mainland, and to **Kent and Erin Matsui,** who welcomed our family to serve alongside them in Hawai'i–thank you for helping us navigate a major life transition. You played a huge role in helping our family adapt and grow, and we will forever be thankful for your guidance.

To **my diverse Hawai'i 'ohana—Alison, Virginia, Emilie, Margarita, Madeleine, Rebecca, Marie, and Sylvi**—who did life with me for six wonderful years. From raising our children together to exploring the Big Island's beauty and discovering new foods, our time together will always hold a special place in my heart.

To **the wonderful homeschool communities** in both Maryland and Hawai'i—thank you for the friendship, encouragement, and shared adventures. The deep sense of community made these years rich and meaningful for our family. Your support and camaraderie during this season of life were a gift.

To **Heather Holleman,** who believed in my writing before I even put pen to paper, your support and encouragement at just the right moments kept me going when I felt like quitting.

To **Hālina Yin,** who patiently answered my many questions about Hawaiian history and culture and who demonstrated true aloha—your insights and kindness meant so much to me.

To **Virginia Dunn,** thank you for your friendship and encouragement throughout our writing journeys. I'll always cherish our time refining our manuscripts together.

To **Kristi Efford,** for your insights and invaluable contributions as a Marriage and Family Therapist to this book—thank you for lending your expertise.

To **the Hilo Public Library,** your extended hours allowed me to focus on my manuscript while our daughters were at evening sports practices, and for that, I'm truly thankful. And when the library was closed, a special shoutout to **Starbucks**—your caffeine (and free Wi-Fi) kept me going during those writing sessions!

To **the team at hope*writers,** thank you for creating a

supportive community that encouraged me through the writing process. I'm grateful to have met many incredible authors through this group.

To **Janna Walkup,** my editor—your guidance has not only helped me grow as a writer but also made my work so much more conversational and engaging. Thank you for your patience with my never-ending questions, and for taking my words and turning them into something even better.

To **Elizabeth McColloch,** for providing a detailed checklist that kept me organized and sane throughout the publishing process.

To **my book launch team,** thank you for your support in helping spread the word about this book. Interacting with you in our Facebook group weekly brought me much joy.

Finally, to **Kristen Neighbarger,** my book launch manager—your behind-the-scenes work and social media guidance were invaluable. I am so grateful for your help in making this dream a reality.

Notes

An Invitation to Turn to Him, Not Them

1. Melissa Dougherty, *Happy Lies: How a Movement You (Probably) Never Heard Of Shaped Our Self-Absorbed World,* (Zondervan Books, 2025), 26.

2. Julie Stewart Williams, *From the Mountains to the Sea: Early Hawaiian Life,* (Kamehameha Schools Bernice Pauahi Bishop Estate, 1997), 117.

Limited Sight Distance

1. Daniel Kikawa, *The True God of Hawai'i: The Case for 'Io* (Aloha Ke Akua Publishing, 2021), 31–32.

2. Daniel Kikawa, *Perpetuated in Righteousness: The Journey of the Hawaiian People from Eden (Kalana I Haulola) to the Present Time,* (Aloha Ke Akua Publishing, 1994), 55.

3. Beth Price-Williams, "10 Hilarious Inside Jokes You'll Only Appreciate If You Hail from Pennsylvania," *Only In Your State,* March 27, 2019, https://www.onlyinyourstate.com/pennsylvania/inside-jokes-pa/

My Invisibility Superpower

1. Whitney Akin, *Overlooked: Finding Your Worth When You Feel All Alone,* (Leafwood Publishers, 2023), 25.

2. Akin, *Overlooked: Finding Your Worth,* 26.

3. Will Hutcherson and Chinwé Williams, *Seen: Healing Despair and Anxiety in Kids and Teens Through the Power of Connection*, (Parent Cue, 2021), 19.

4. Vivek H. Murthy, *Our Epidemic of Loneliness and Isolation: The U.S. Surgeon General's Advisory on the Healing Effects of Social Connection and Community,* (Office of the U.S. Surgeon General, 2023), 4.

5. Guy Winch, "10 Surprising Facts About Rejection," *Psychology Today,* July 3, 2013, https://www.psychology today.com/us/blog/the-squeaky-wheel/201307/10-surprising-facts-about-rejection

6. Gary Chapman, *Seen. Known. Loved.: 5 Truths about God and Your Love Language*, (Northfield Publishing, 2020), 7.

7. Chapman, *Seen. Known. Loved.*, 13.

8. David A. Seamands, *Healing for Damaged Emotions: Recovering from the Memories That Cause Our Pain*, (David C. Cook, 1991), 39-40, 46.

9. Rich Schmidt, "Did God Really Turn His Face Away While Jesus Was on the Cross?" *Rich Schmidt* (blog), April 24, 2020, https://richschmidt.org/blog/did-god-turn-his-face-away

The God Who Sees

1. Dale Ralph Davis, *Faith of our Father: Expositions of Genesis 12-25* (Christian Focus Publications LTD, 2015), 69. This move is repeated by Sarah's grandson's wife, Rachel, when she cannot conceive.

2. Dale Ralph Davis, *Faith of our Father*, 75.

3. Bruce K. Waltke and Cathi J. Fredricks, *Genesis: A Commentary* (Zondervan Academic, 2001), 254.

4. John Temple Bristow, *What Paul Really Said about Women: An Apostle's Liberating Views on Equality in Marriage, Leadership, and Love* (HarperSanFrancisco, 1988), 19.

5. Victor P. Hamilton, *The Book of Genesis (The New International Commentary on the Old Testament): Chapters 1-17* (Grand Rapids: Wm B Eerdmans, 1990), 444.

6. Tasha Jun, *Tell Me the Dream Again: Reflections on Family, Ethnicity & the Sacred Work of Belonging* (Tyndale, 2023), 8.

Living for One Gaze

1. Michelle Faverio and Olivia Sidoti, "Teens, Social Media and Technology 2024." *Pew Research Center,* December 12, 2024. https://www.pewresearch.org/internet/2024/12/12/teens-social-media-and-technology-2024/

2. Brittany Maher and Cassandra Speer, *Her Truth Worth: Breaking Free From a Culture of Selfies, Side Hustles, and People Pleasing to Embrace Your True Identity in Christ* (Nelson Books, 2022), 41.

3. Brittany Maher and Cassandra Speer, *Her True Worth,* 66.

4. Hosanna Wong, *You Are More Than You've Been Told: Unlock a Fresh Way to Live Through the Rhythms of Jesus* (W Publishing Group, 2023), 40.

5. Two tremendous middle-grade books addressing this topic are Heather Holleman's *This Seat's Saved* (Moody, 2023) and the sequel *The Disappearing Seat* (Moody, 2025).

6. "Nainoa Thompson Special Lecture on the Hōkūle'a and Native Hawaiian Health (May 23, 2016)," *National Library of Medicine,* last modified December 6, 2019, https://www.nlm.nih.gov/news/Hokulea_Lecture.html

7. David Hess, "Trust is a Must" (sermon, Christ Community Church, Camp Hill, PA, June 4, 2023).

8. Matt Chandler, "The God of Mercy and Glory," *The Village Church,* filmed April 23, 2017, video, 20:40, https://www.thevillagechurch.net/resources/sermons/the-god-of-mercy-and-glory

When Feelings Take the Wheel

1. Louie Giglio, *Indescribable: 100 Devotions about God and Science* (Nashville: Thomas Nelson, 2017), 187.

2. Loren Cunningham, *Is That Really You, God?: Hearing the Voice of God* (Seattle: YWAM Publishing, 2001), 202.

3. Shannon Messenger, *Nightfall* (New York: Aladdin, 2017), 667-668.

4. My Apologetics professor, Dr. Keith Plummer, used the example of suppressing a beach ball in reference to Romans 1:18, where Paul writes that the unrighteous suppress the truth about what can be known about God.

5. I recommend Melissa Dougherty's *Happy Lies: How a Movement You (Probably) Never Heard Of Shaped Our Self-Absorbed World.* Melissa shares her experience in chapter 5 of being a thirteen-year-old girl who grieved over being a girl and provides insights into today's identity crisis.

6. Kayla Lin, "Using a Feelings Wheel: Why It's Helpful and How It Works," *Parent Cue,* accessed January 7, 2024, https://theparentcue.org/using-a-feelings-wheel-why-its-helpful-and-how-it-works/

7. Will Hutcherson and Chinwé Williams, *Seen: Healing Despair and Anxiety in Kids and Teens Through the Power of Connection* (Parent Cue, 2021), 40-41.

8. Aaron Karmin, "How Long Does the Fight or Flight Reaction Last?" *Psych Central,* June 3, 2016, https://psychcentral.com/blog/anger/2016/06/how-long-does-the-fight-or-flight-reaction-last#1

9. Bill Bright, *Have You Heard of the 4 Spiritual Laws?* Bright Media Foundation and Campus Crusade for Christ, Int., 1965-2013.

10. "Why Many Young Adults Quit," *Christianity Today/Leadership Journal,* October 1, 2007, https://www.christianitytoday.com/pastors/2007/fall/10.15.html

11. Hillary Morgan Ferrer, *Mama Bear Apologetics: Empowering Your Kids to Challenge Cultural Lies* (Eugene: Harvest House Publishers, 2019), 171.

12. Jen Wilkin, *Women of the Word: How to Study the Bible with Both Our Hearts and Our Minds* (Wheaton: Crossway, 2014), 41-42.

13. Wilkin, *Women of the Word,* 42.

14. Cunningham, *Is That Really You?,* 175.

15. Kristi Efford, MFT, provided these instructions for use with the Feelings Wheel.

Forcing Our Way Through Life

1. If you mentor or parent a young person, I highly recommend Jessica L. Peck's *Behind Closed Doors* (Thomas Nelson, 2022). This guide offers professional advice, conversation keys, devotional readings, and writing prompts to support meaningful, relationship-building conversations at home.

Stressing ≠ Solving

1. Serena Menken writes books and articles that capture the unique moments of gut-wrenching pain and heartfelt joy experienced by parents of teens with mental health concerns. Connect with her at https://serenamenken.substack.com

2. A. J. Adams, "It's OK to Not Be OK," *Psychology Today,* May 20, 2020, https://www.psychologytoday.com/us/blog/flourish/202005/its-ok-not-be-ok

3. Guy Winch, "10 Crucial Differences Between Worry and Anxiety," *Psychology Today,* March 14, 2016, https:/www.psychologytoday.com/us/blog/the-squeaky-wheel/2016 03/10-crucial-differences-between-worry-and-anxiety

4. Steph Coelho, "Am I Worried or Anxious? Here's the Difference," *PsychCentral,* August 8, 2022, https://www.psychcentral.com/anxiety/worry-vs-anxiety

5. Linda Dillow, *Calm My Anxious Heart: A Woman's Guide to Finding Contentment* (NavPress, 1998), 116.

6. "G3308 - merimna - Strong's Greek Lexicon (esv)," *Blue Letter Bible,* accessed November 9, 2023, https://www.blueletterbible.org/lexicon/g3308/esv/mgnt/0-1/

7. "G3309 - merimnaō - Strong's Greek Lexicon (esv)," *Blue Letter Bible,* accessed November 9, 2023, https://www.blueletterbible.org/lexicon/g3309/esv/mgnt/0-1/

Flirting with Spiritual Darkness

1. Emily P. Freeman, *The Next Right Thing: A Simple, Soulful Practice for Making Life Decisions* (Revell, 2019), 16.

2. Jezebel practiced sorcery (2 Kings 9:22). Burning his son as an offering, King Manassah used fortune-telling and omens and dealt with mediums and necromancers (2 Kings 21:6).

3. Herb Kawainui Kāne, "The 'Aumakua—Hawaiian Ancestral Spirits," *State of Hawaii,* accessed June 19, 2021, https://dlnr.hawaii.gov/sharks/files/2014/07/APaperbyHerbKane.pdf

4. Charles Montgomery, *The Shark God: Encounters with Ghosts and Ancestors in the South Pacific* (University of Chicago Press, 2007).

5. Daniel Kikawa, "Spiritus Article #1," (Academic Paper, 2004), 5.

Carrying the Spirit with Confidence

1. "Life Challenges," *EveryStudent.com,* accessed March 21, 2023, https://www.everystudent.com/menus/enigmas.html

2. Danny Desin, "Danny Desin: Sport is a Metaphor for Life," *Montana Sports,* accessed April 20, 2023, https://www.montanasports.com/high-school/danny-desin-sport-is-a-metaphor-for-life

3. Judges 6:34, 1 Chronicles 12:18-19, 2 Chronicles 24:20.

4. Meredith Kline, *Images of the Spirit* (Grand Rapids: Baker Book House Company, 1980), 58.

5. I first heard this illustration from Cru staff and student leaders during my time at Towson University, though I'm unsure of its original source.

6. Liza Kobayashi, *A Deeper Relationship with Holy Spirit* (Independently published, 2021), 14-15.

7. Scott Crocker, "Holy Spirit Terminology," *Cru,* accessed May 1, 2023, https://www.cru.org/us/en/train-and-grow/ spiritual-growth/core-christian-beliefs/theological- perspective-on-the-holy-spirit.3.html

Restoring Your Connection with God

1. "75 Motivational Mantras to Help You Succeed in Life," *Basics by Becca* (blog), January 19, 2022, https://www. basicsbybecca.com/blog/motivational-mantras

2. WTRF. "Former Addict, Prisoner Turned Motivational Speaker Meets with Belmont County Students." *WTRF*, November 20, 2024, https://www.wtrf.com/top-stories/ former-addict-prisoner-turned-motivational-speaker- meets-with-belmont-county-students/

3. Timothy Keller, *The Meaning of Marriage: Facing the Complexities of Commitment with the Wisdom of God* (Dutton, 2011), 95.

4. "Ten Fun Facts about Brett Favre," *Ten Facts About,* accessed March 28, 2023, https://www.10-facts-about. com/brett-favre/id/1236

Overcoming the Opposition with the Holy Spirit

1. The *her.BIBLE* app is available on the App Store or on Google Play. Learn more at https://her.bible/app/

2. Heather Holleman and Ashley Holleman, *Sent: Living a Life That Invites Others to Jesus* (Moody, 2021), Introduction, Kindle.

Please leave Tracy a
Review

If this book encouraged or helped you in any way, would you take a moment to leave a review? Your words can help another young woman find this message at just the right time

SCAN ME
SCAN ME
SCAN ME
SCAN ME

★★★★★

You don't need to write a long review—just a sentence or two sharing how the book impacted you is more than enough!

www.fromhimnotthem.com/review

ABOUT THE AUTHOR

TRACY HARPER is a speaker, teacher, and writer with over twenty years of experience in campus ministry. Her journey has taken her from the Eastern United States to Hawaii, where she *somehow* managed to do ministry in a place filled with sunshine, rainbows, and students from around the world. She has a bachelor's degree in Secondary Education/English from Towson University and has completed Cru's Institute of Biblical Studies program. Tracy is married, has three daughters, and lives in Maryland. where she now enjoys life near the water— preferably with a good book and a great cup of coffee.

	www.tracyharperwrites.com
	TracyHarperWrites
	TracyHarperWrites
	Tracy Harper

Visit **www.tracyharperwrites.com** to sign up for Tracy's monthly devotions that help women reset their relationship with God, self, and others.